The Niche Threat
Deterring the Use of
Chemical and Biological Weapons

The Niche Threat
Deterring the Use of
Chemical and Biological Weapons

Edited by
Stuart E. Johnson

1997

National Defense University Press
Washington, DC

National Defense University Press Publications

To increase general knowledge and inform discussion, the Institute for National Strategic Studies, through its publication arm the NDU Press, publishes *Strategic Forums*; McNair Papers; proceedings of University- and Institute-sponsored symposia; books relating to U.S. national security, especially to issues of joint, combined, or coalition warfare, peacekeeping operations, and national strategy; and a variety of other works designed to circulate contemporary comment and offer alternatives to current policy. The Press occasionally publishes out-of-print defense classics, historical works, and other especially timely or distinguished writing on national security.

NDU Press publications are sold by the U.S. Government Printing Office. For ordering information, call (202) 512-1800 or write to the Superintendent of Documents, U.S. Government Printing Office, Washington, DC 20402.

Library of Congress Cataloging-in-Publication Data
The niche threat : deterring the use of chemical and biological weapons / edited by Stuart E. Johnson.
    p. cm.
    Includes bibliographical references.
    1. Weapons of mass destruction. 2. Arms race. 3. United States—Military policy.
  4. Deterrence (Strategy) I. Johnson, Stuart. E., 1944-
    U793.N53   1996
    327.1'745—dc21   96-39958
                                                  CIP

First Printing, February 1997

ISBN 0-16-054403-3

Contents

Preface

The problem of chemical and biological weapons of mass destruction is not well understood by the general public nor, for that matter, by the members of the Armed Forces who could face these terrible weapons first should they be unleashed by a rogue nation or terrorist group—or even by accident

Complicating this lack of understanding is the ironic reality that use of chemical and biological—and even limited nuclear—weapons has become a greater threat than it was in the Cold War era, when the superpowers kept a leash on their client states. Now, nations that cannot hope to challenge the United States seriously with conventional force have the means and possibly the motivation to use such weapons. Iraq comes to mind as a prominent example. The authors of this volume have coined the term "niche threat" to identify these states, falling as they do in a category below major power status but above the threshhold of WMD capability.

While civilized nations have repudiated the use of such weapons, we must confront the possibility of having to deter and defend against chemical and biological weapons. Accordingly, the essays in this collection discuss the dangers of the niche threat, the possibility that such weapons could be used, and the measures the United States can employ to deter their use.

The Niche Threat
Deterring the Use of
Chemical and Biological Weapons

✦ *Introduction:*
The Rise of the WMD "Niche" Threat

STUART E. JOHNSON

The end of the Cold War has had a number of unintended consequences that have presented U.S. policy-makers with difficult choices. None has been more difficult than confronting the spread of "WMD," or "weapons of mass destruction." The framework of superpower rivalry between Washington and Moscow that provided a measure of restraint on client states is gone. More and more states—former client states and other states as well—are seeking such weaponry. Particularly troubling is the rise of the "niche" threat, a term coined to refer to that category of states who lack the conventional power to challenge the United States, but who do possess the resources and know-how to possibly resort to WMD, especially biological or chemical weapons. Today, some 20 nations appear to have biological or chemical weapons development programs (or both).

Stuart Johnson edited this collection while he was Director of Strategy and Policy Analysis, Institute for National Strategic Studies, National Defense University, Washington, DC.

The United States is still feeling its way in coping with this new environment. We had tended to view the challenge of weapons of mass destruction in the context of the Cold War, in which the capability of mutual assured destruction residing in the United States and Soviet Union provided the overarching framework for much of our policy-making. This deterrence framework was relatively well established and though it underwent constant refinement in the decades of the 60s, 70s, and 80s, the rules of the game were well understood. Chemical and biological weapons were regarded in large part as lesser included cases in this broader deterrent policy. The end of the Cold War should have made our national security choices simpler. Gone, or at least greatly diminished, is the most troublesome threat to U.S. national security, the global competition with the Soviet Union, a peer superpower. Moreover, Moscow no longer has the wherewithal or intent to challenge us head-on with conventional forces in areas of critical interest to the United States.

This goes for the rest of the world as well. U.S. forces are far more capable relative to plausible adversaries than at any other time since the onset of the Cold War. Our forces are better trained and better equipped than anyone we are likely to meet on the battlefield and time is on our side in a number of critical areas:

- The military equipment stock of the North Korean army is aging and becoming more obsolescent with every passing year. Moreover, its lack of hard currency and loss of sizable arms transfers from Beijing and Moscow make prospects for renewing its capital stock increasingly remote. Shortages of POL (petroleum, oil, and lubricants in military parlance) have limited severely the amount the forces can train, making a classical conventional invasion of the South increasingly uncertain.
- The Iraqi military of 1996 is not the Iraqi military of 1990 that invaded Kuwait. It too has suffered from a lack of access to modern military equipment and, though not in the straits that

North Korea finds itself in, is struggling with the effects of a half decade of economic embargo.

● The overall trend in defense spending has been downward and the arms transfers from Russia to Third World nations are one-tenth of what they were a decade ago. This means that, overall, stocks of equipment in Third World armies potentially hostile to U.S. interests are aging or declining (or both).

Still, a dark cloud looms over these otherwise favorable trends: the spread of weapons of mass destruction. The removal of the superpower rivalry that provided a constraining framework is coupled with the growing availability of the requisite technology to any nation with a moderate amount of hard currency and a persistent determination to acquire such weaponry. And, ironically, as conventional arms become more expensive, weapons of mass destruction become an attractive alternative for influencing the balance of power among nations in a region. Hence, Pakistan is strongly motivated to have a credible nuclear weapons capability, in part to neutralize India's possession of the same and in part to offset the much larger conventional forces that India can field. India, in turn, has the same motives as it watches the larger Chinese military that includes larger, more capable nuclear forces.

These circumstances have been with us for over a decade now. While they are still worrisome, a growing concern is the nation that cannot hope to challenge the United States with conventional weapons on the battlefield, but sees an opportunity to gain leverage over us or our partners by posing this "niche" threat. Short of defeating us on the battlefield, a nation possessing weapons of mass destruction could complicate considerably our ability to operate in key regions far from our shores. The threat of employment of chemical or biological weaponry would raise the risk of U.S. deployments possibly enough to tilt an uncertain deliberation away from deployment. The actual employment of chemical or biological weaponry would raise the cost of a U.S. deployment and present difficult response choices to the president. For this purpose, nuclear weaponry is not required. Chemical and biological weaponry, easier to afford and easier to develop clandestinely, can suffice. The WMD niche threat can change the context of a U.S. deployment dramatically. Where the U.S. military would ordinarily be able to dominate most theaters and act with virtual impunity, weapons of mass destruction in the hands of a local adversary would force the national command authorities to think long and hard before exposing U.S. forces to such a risk.

It is this "niche" threat, the use of chemical or biological weaponry, that has grown in concern in recent years. In the minds of some theater commanders, it is the more likely threat and therefore deserves the same level of attention as the threat of proliferation of nuclear weapons. The Chairman of the Joint Chiefs of Staff, recognizing the challenges that the niche threat poses, asked a number of scholars to develop a set of proposals on how to think differently about the threat. This volume contains the views of four noted authors who responded to the Chairman's call.

The concern on the part of the Department of Defense is not new. Indeed it has gained considerable attention in recent years. The most prominent response has been the Co-operative Threat Reduction program initiated in 1991 through which the United States has assisted the nuclear weapons holding states of the former Soviet Union to dismantle, transport, store, and secure their nuclear warheads. From the perspective of preventing the spread of nuclear weapons, efforts to improve the physical protection and the control and accounting of fissile material have become critical. Programs to improve our defenses against chemical and biological weapons (CBW) are also underway. These are in response to deficiencies in our CBW capabilities that were revealed during operation Desert Storm. Finally, the current administration plan would provide about $14 billion for ballistic missile defense programs over the next five years. This represents a "goal line stand" approach: if all else fails and launch takes place, it gives us, at a high cost, the ability to provide our troops and our allies in the conflict region a measure of protection.

But there is only so much the United States can do through these programs. Ultimately, nations will decide whether to pursue acquisition of weapons of mass destruction based on fundamental issues of national security that have always shaped such decisions. We are concerned here with the need to provide the appropriate mix of incentives and disincentives to nations to dissuade them from acquiring, or, if they already possess the weapons, from expanding their arsenal or actually employing them. It is this approach—*deterring* WMD—that our authors address in their chapters.

In the first chapter, Brad Roberts discusses the need to establish a new set of assumptions for framing U.S. CBW planning. In the new global environment, he asserts that the scenarios for CBW use against U.S. forces have actually expanded far beyond what was thought probable during the Cold War. Roberts also explores how, under certain conditions, CBW may become the equalizer vis-a-vis the United States.

In the next chapter, Jerome Kahan provides an overview of the NBC environment today and its implications for U.S. forces abroad. He explores the options and the parameters for U.S. retaliation against a state which employs WMD against American troops. Kahan also discusses how the United States could employ a comprehensive array of countermeasures against an NBC attack and the adjustments which should be made in U.S. doctrine and training.

Keith Payne follows with a theoretical analysis of what deterrence has traditionally meant and the impact of the changing environment on the field. His behaviorist approach identifies options for U.S. deterrence strategies today. One of the main difficulties facing planners today is how to effectively communicate to potential adversaries that the U.S. response is not only credible, but likely devastating. Payne concludes with a recommendation that the United States pursue a policy of "denial deterrence" rather than "punitive deterrence."

Leon Sloss concludes with another perspective of the issue of deterrence by arguing that it should be employed at all junctures: from the pre-acquisition stage to wartime employment of WMD. He is a strong advocate of expanding intelligence-gathering to provide U.S. planners with an in-depth understanding of what motivates the societies of potential adversaries and how they would perceive U.S. efforts at deterrence. Sloss provides a comprehensive discussion of how best to influence an adversary's perceptions.

These papers were prepared at the request of the Chairman of the Joint Chiefs of Staff who felt that, as valuable as U.S. programs on nonproliferation and counterproliferation were, more focus needed to be placed on chemical and biological weaponry. Our counterproliferation efforts have appropriately focused primarily on programs that target the proliferation of nuclear weaponry. These are often, but not always, effective in countering chemical and biological weaponry as well. The theater commanders-in-chief recognized first-hand the potential problems of possession of chemical and biological weaponry by smaller nations in their regions. Their concerns about thinking through the WMD niche threat were appropriately communicated to the Chairman, Joint Chiefs of Staff, and a search for new approaches was launched. I hope the ideas presented here will not only prove useful in their own right, but will stimulate further analysis and discussion of this issue that is key to our defense planning.

✦ Between Panic and Complacency:
Calibrating the Chemical and Biological Warfare Problem

BRAD ROBERTS

After the near brush with chemical and biological warfare in the Persian Gulf War, such weapons attracted sudden attention from military leaders and security analysts. Five years later, interest has dissipated. It is unfortunate but true that the nuclear and conventional weapons of potential U.S. adversaries have received a good deal more attention than their chemical and biological counterparts in terms of their impact on regional security dynamics and U.S. military operations. The concern about chemical and biological weapons (CBW) has waned for a variety of reasons—some dismiss the concern as a panicky overreaction; others avoid the problem because it simply seems too hard. Complacency again grips the policy community. The results could be catastrophic.

Brad Roberts is a member of the professional staff of the Institute for Defense Analyses. He was formerly editor of *The Washington Quarterly* and a research fellow at the Center for Strategic and International Studies. The author is grateful for valuable comments on earlier drafts by Seth Carus, Graham Pearson, and Victor Utgoff.

Between panic and complacency, how should the risk best be understood? The purpose of this paper is to calibrate the chemical and biological warfare problem as it exists today and as it can reasonably be expected to evolve over the next decade. It seeks to answer the following questions: In what ways do these weapons matter? In what ways do they *not* matter? *How* do they matter? How not? The paper begins with a survey of the proliferation problem. It turns to a review of the scenarios of CBW use by U.S. adversaries. An assessment of the military and political implications of CBW proliferation for U.S. security strategies more generally is then offered. The paper concludes with a discussion of challenges to the planning assumptions that underpin current policy.

The Proliferation Problem

Chemical weapons emerged in the 1980s as a major proliferation concern. The number of states allegedly possessing chemical weapons has grown steadily in recent years, with approximately a doubling of states in the last three decades.[1] Six countries possessed or actively sought offensive chemical warfare (CW) capabilities from 1945 to 1960, 7 in the 1960s, about 13 in the 1970s, and about 16 by 1984.[2] In 1990, the then-director of U.S. naval intelligence, Rear Admiral Thomas A. Brooks, testified to a subcommittee of the House Armed Services Committee that:

> at least fourteen countries outside of NATO and the Warsaw Pact currently have an offensive chemical warfare capability. Many of these nations are likely to assist other countries in developing offensive capabilities as well. Ten more nations are believed to be either developing (or are suspected of seeking) an offensive CW capability.[3]

He identified those that "probably possess" chemical weapons as China, Egypt, India, Iran, Iraq, Israel, Libya, Myanmar, North Korea,

Pakistan, South Korea, Syria, Taiwan, and Vietnam. He also identified Indonesia, Saudi Arabia, South Africa, and Thailand as countries that "may possess" such weapons.

There may in fact be significant variations in the chemical warfare capabilities of these nations. Some states may actually possess chemical weapons while others may only be engaged in a research and development (R&D) program aimed at possible future acquisition. Some reports refer simply to "CW capable" states, which might reasonably include many states with the industrial infrastructure, expertise, and access to materials necessary for the production of CW agents. Moreover, such reports indicate nothing about the military significance of the CW programs of the accused states. The military utility of toxic chemical agent is a direct function of the quantity and quality available, its mating with effective delivery systems, and the military capability to use—and exploit the use of—chemical weapons in war. The thresholds of quantity and quality vary with circumstance—what one state might find threatening another might dismiss as inconsequential. The U.S. Government itself has been unclear on this point, with one official indicating in January 1989 that perhaps as few as five or six states might possess arsenals of chemical weapons of clear military significance.[4] The problem with the publicly available data is that they permit no study of these factors.[5]

Biological weapons may emerge as the principal proliferation concern of the next decade. Reports indicate that 11 countries are pursuing offensive-oriented biological warfare programs, up from just 4 in the 1960s (of which 2 were the United States and the USSR).[6] Those publicly identified by U.S. Government sources include Iraq, Iran, Syria, Libya, China, North Korea, and Taiwan.[7] U.S. officials have also made a general statement that of those suspected of pursuing biological warfare (BW) programs, some are in the Middle East, some are known sponsors of terrorism, and some are signatories of the Biological and Toxin Weapons Convention (BWC).[8]

The number of states engaged in BW programs with offensive applications could well be larger, because officials have underscored that evidence of proscribed activities has been uncovered virtually randomly and not as a result of a systematic survey. BW R&D programs aimed at offensive uses are extremely challenging intelligence targets and absence of evidence cannot readily be interpreted as evidence of absence. Reports of efforts to acquire from Russian sources the expertise to produce biological weapons—and even the weapons themselves—have surfaced in the Russian press.[9]

Discovery of Iraq's BW program helped to awaken interest in the biological aspects of the proliferation problem.[10] But the continuing debate within the UN Special Commission on Iraq (UNSCOM) about the character and scale of Iraq's BW program echoes a similar debate in the chemical area: What are the implications of simple statements about numbers of proliferators? Are all proliferators of equal significance?

The apparent basis of the proliferation assessment for specific countries is the evaluation that activities are being carried out that do not appear to be for permitted peaceful purposes. Such findings may derive from discovery of quantities of infective materials for which no peaceful purposes are discernible. As in the nuclear and chemical areas, a certain type of proliferation ladder exists. Steps along the way to a full-blown military capability to use chemical and biological weapons for offensive purposes start with R&D and proceed to the proofing of weapon concepts, test production, scaling up of production capability, stockpiling of agent, acquisition of dissemination equipment (in the case of BW), weaponization of agents (largely in the case of CW), stockpiling of weapons, preparation of delivery systems, creation of the doctrine for use, and training. A sophisticated CBW program would probably also entail the acquisition of and training with protective measures; not every developing country will share the military and public safety concerns of the developed world, but many will find some protective measures prudent if only to preserve secrecy in the BW domain by preventing health problems that might otherwise be detected. In the R&D phase of a BW program itself, there are important differences between programs that emphasize the relatively simple agents that were the focus of interest among the superpowers prior to their agreement to the BWC and the novelties made possible by bioengineering. Of course, even a stockpile or capability deemed to be fairly rudimentary can be militarily significant in certain circumstances and thus is not to be dismissed lightly.

The widespread tendency in the research and policy communities to equate the military significance of different unconventional weapons can lead to a serious misunderstanding of the character and impact of different weapons programs in the developing world. Chemical and biological weapons are less predictable in their effects than are nuclear weapons, given their vulnerability to meteorological conditions and protective measures and, in the case of tactical use of chemical weapons, the need for near-perfect delivery on target. Moreover, there are also important differences between chemical and biological weapons, with the former requiring large quantities for decisive battlefield effect (in order to sustain lethal dosages) and the latter being ill-suited for battlefield use (given the delay arising from periods of incubation associated with most agents). Biological weapons in particular are potentially devastating against large population concentrations. But even in very low quantities, both operate quite effectively as weapons of terror. Moreover, even these generalizations can be grossly misleading. Tactical applications of biological weapons are by no means inconceivable. And strategic uses of even relatively small quantities of chemical agents, especially delivered by aircraft or ballistic or cruise missiles against cities, must also be taken into account. Moreover, the line between tactical and strategic is not always clear.

The specific attributes of a country's capabilities are also relevant. Factors such as the quantity and quality of available weapons or stockpiles of CW or BW agents, the industrial capacity to surge production in time of war, the accuracy of delivery systems, and the maturity of military doctrine and adequacy of training will bear significantly on the character of the military risk posed by such systems. One of the most disturbing aspects of the proliferation problem of the 1990s is the apparent increasing sophistication of many of the chemical and biological proliferators as their national capacities in each of these areas grow more robust. An important question, probably answerable only with intelligence information, is the degree to which these national programs are creating war-ready and war-winning capabilities against even advanced and well-protected conventional forces. In the chemical domain and in scenarios involving attack on U.S. forces, the requirements for such a capability are considerable. In the biological domain, the requirements are less substantial.

Within the intelligence community, the task of diagnosing the BW threat sometimes falls prey to some old ways of thinking. There is a natural tendency, especially within a military community accustomed to building weapons to stockpile them for deterrence purposes, to dismiss the significance of chemical and biological weapons programs that have deliberately chosen not to produce stockpiles of weapons or agents. This is a tendency that leads to a dangerous misreading of the proliferation dynamic. Iraq's chemical weapons program in the 1990s was designed to build and distribute such weapons for immediate use on the battlefield; it was a classic surge capability, held in reserve by a state intending to use weapons not to deter but to fight and win. An important intelligence challenge arises from the predisposition to look for chemical and biological warfare agents of the kind produced by the United States until the ban in 1969, which were often chosen because of their long-term stability in storage, rather than for those abandoned because of their instability.

Moreover, in the case of biological warfare agents, weaponization is hardly necessary—convenient perhaps for some agents, but not necessary. Because the quantity of agent required to be effective against a military target is small, relatively few delivery systems are necessary. Furthermore, effective dissemination is possible through simple spray systems.

Against this backdrop, it is hardly reassuring to note that the technology, materials, and expertise to produce chemical and biological weapons are widely diffused internationally. Any state with a petrochemical or fertilizer industry can make chemical warfare agents. Any state with medical research facilities or any fermentation-based industry can make biological warfare agents. As the process of global industrialization and economic integration unfolds further, more and more advanced technologies will be in the hands of an ever larger number of states. The point here is not to trivialize the problem; rather, it is to focus on the latent capacities in most states and the decisions involved in assembling the ingredients of an offensive war-fighting capability in the chemical and biological domains.

Military significance is also a function of circumstance. The CW and BW capabilities of states of the developing world may be strategic in conflict against similarly sized competitors in their region if they can be used to achieve massively destructive effects or to tilt the political dynamic of conflict in favor of one side or another. The threat of their use will then operate powerfully on the perceived choices of the targeted nation's leaders. Not all of the CW or BW capabilities of the rumored proliferators are likely to meet this criterion, although this will also be a function of the defense capabilities of the attacked states. Moreover, against states of the developed world, the threat of the use of chemical weapons would likely have only limited consequences. The military forces of such states, if capable of fighting in a chemically contaminated environment in a sound protective posture in the form of effective personal protective gear, detectors, and decontamination gear, should find a chemical attack little more than a hindrance, except in circumstances when such an attack can be massed or sustained for long periods. In the case of biological weapons, however, even small arsenals are likely to operate with profound effect on the choices of leaders of both small and powerful nations given their credible potential for massive devastation.

This illustrates the role of defenses in shaping the risk posed by offensive chemical and biological warfare capabilities. Strong and effective preventive- and counter-measures diminish significantly the utility of an opponent's chemical and biological warfare capabilities. Two caveats are important, however. First, a perfect defense that negates an opponent's advantages is impossible, and improvements to defensive capability should be understood as relevant to driving up thresholds of military utility, but not eliminating them. This is especially true when one factors in the possibility that civilian as well as military targets may be attacked with such weapons. Second, the burdensome effects of protective gear may prove an Achilles' heel for the attacked force as its degrading effects on combat operations take their cumulative toll. These effects will result specifically in those cases where an opponent can mimic the chemical warfare capabilities of the erstwhile Warsaw Pact in terms of comprehensive and sustained chemical attack, in which agent types were matched to specific targets and delivered with high accuracy, and targets were periodically reattacked to sustain lethal dosages. But these caveats should not distract decision makers from the essential benefits of strong and effective protective measures and countermeasures.

The purpose of this digression on military utility is to illustrate the important differences that exist among those weapons so often lumped into the general category of "unconventional weapons" or "weapons of mass destruction." Given the unfamiliarity of many analysts with chemical and biological weapons, there is a tendency to equate these weapons with their nuclear counterparts in terms of their military and political weight. There is a similar tendency to equate R&D programs in terms of their strategic significance; but the differences among these weapons and programs are as important as their similarities.

Furthermore, whatever the utility of chemical and biological weapons from a U.S. point of view and for U.S. military purposes, it would be dangerous to believe that all other states will view that utility or take military/political decisions in similar fashion. A lesson from the domain of chemical weapons proliferation is worth noting here: Iraq's use of chemical weapons in its war against Iran caused many developing countries to question whether the conventional wisdoms of the West about chemical weapons, born of their unique experience in World War I, were relevant on non-European battlefields. The result of this questioning was a spurt of chemical weapons proliferation, contrary to the expectations of many in the U.S. military community who believed such weapons to be anachronistic and of little more than nuisance value.

Looking at the future, biological weapons are likely to emerge as a much greater concern for the U.S. military than chemical weapons. Far smaller quantities are needed and can be disseminated effectively using commercial sprayers. And in a world where the acquisition of nuclear weapons is politically costly and difficult to do covertly, where chemical weapons have been outlawed under the new Chemical Weapons Convention with its intrusive verification system, and where conventional militaries capable of defeating the advanced countries will be prohibitively expensive, biological weapons capabilities held in reserve may be the option of choice for a state with a perceived need for a strategic capability. This option may seem all the more appealing given the dual-use nature of the materials and technologies suited to a BW program and given the absence of verification and compliance provisions in the global disarmament treaty, the Biological and Toxin Weapons Convention.

Moreover, from a scientific and technical point of view, many of the perceptions about the military utility of biological weapons are increasingly unsound. The understanding of biological weapons prevalent within the U.S. military is based on the technology of the 1940s, 1950s, and 1960s. Since the United States abandoned an offensive biological warfare capability in 1969, there has been a revolution in the biological sciences at least as profound as the one in physics that led to the splitting of the atom. Biotechnology's impact on biological warfare has been overdramatized by some. For the moment, the biotechnology revolution has led not to the creation of novel, highly lethal biowarfare agents, but rather to an easing of the technical factors that heretofore have made such weapons time-consuming to produce, risky to store, and difficult to control on the battlefield. In the long term, however, the mapping of the human genome, combined with the ability to manipulate genetic material, offer the prospect of weapons targeted against specific races or other genetically identifiable groups. Such technologies may also help on the defensive side, with the production of polyvalent vaccines, effective against a range of BW agents, or broadband, prompt medical treatment that reduces the utility of biological attack. At the very least, the biotechnology revolution is rapidly diffusing the technology, materials, and expertise necessary to exploit its benefits for human health and agricultural purposes—and thereby creating a latent warfare capability.

But this emphasis on biological weapons should not distract attention from the chemical threat. Chemical weapons appear to be more broadly proliferated, better integrated into the militaries of the developing world, and "normalized" as an instrument of war there as a result of the Iran-Iraq war of the 1980s.

Challenges to Military Operations

To gain a better understanding of the challenges to U.S. military operations posed by such weapons, it is useful to identify different threat scenarios.

During the Cold War, two basic scenarios dominated U.S. thinking about the possible role of chemical and biological weapons.

(1) *Strategic use*: From early World War II into the Cold War, the primary concern about possible attack on the United States with biological weapons was in strategic applications, i.e., in attacks on U.S. cities. Chemical weapons were essentially dismissed from this scenario. It was believed that Japan and perhaps Germany and later the Soviet Union were prepared to wage such warfare, and the United States sought retaliatory capabilities.

But during World War II, biological weapons were not used for such purposes and first high explosives, then fire-bombing, and finally the atomic bomb came to dominate U.S. thinking about strategic war. The 1969 decision to abandon biological weapons reflected at least in part an assessment that a strategic BW capability was redundant in a U.S. arsenal dominated by nuclear weapons and that the United States did not need to retain a capacity to threaten retaliation in kind in order to deter biological attack on the United States.

In the next decade, biological weapons may again come to be seen by some states as a way to threaten massively destructive attacks on U.S. population centers in a total war situation. This scenario is rated unlikely but not impossible. Used for these purposes, however, biological weapons could indeed be massively destructive, causing a scale of death and casualty comparable to if not greater than that of nuclear weapons.

(2) *Tactical use*: During this same period, chemical weapons were conceived in strictly tactical terms. Especially in Europe, their role in a Warsaw Pact strategy to control the pace and character of a high tempo armored confrontation was widely understood. NATO supported a doctrine of retaliation in kind, with the United States as the sole chemically armed NATO member by the 1960s. Attention to the specific war-winning advantages embodied in the Pact's chemical capability was galvanized in the early 1980s as greater

appreciation emerged of the level of investment and preparation made by Pact forces, which NATO then had a difficult time matching. But in tactical applications outside the European theater, chemical weapons evoked scant interest.

On the biological side, there was some consideration during this period of the utility of biological weapons in tactical applications, such as against naval task forces, amphibious operations, the attack of rear areas, and logistics concentrations. Although it is perceived that the slowness with which biological weapons produce their effects limits their utility in the direct contact battle, toxins take little longer than mustard gas to have effect. Moreover, this slowness presents no difficulty for the attack of rear area targets and other tactical targets identified above. Biological weapons are well suited to the attack of targets of campaign significance, i.e., targets whose loss will cause a change to the outcome of the campaign.

In the next decade, the view of biological weapons as ill-suited for tactical applications may change. The view derives, after all, from the misunderstanding of the technical attributes of BW agents noted above. Moreover, the suitability of biological weapons for the attack of targets of campaign significance may actually increase. Biotechnology may yet produce a biological agent whose effect on humans is sufficiently rapid to give it credible battlefield utility. Its immediate effect seems to be to make it much easier to produce rapidly and in large quantities toxins and other fast-acting poisons. Poisons such as curare are well known and arguably should be regarded as biological warfare agents.

These two scenarios have dominated U.S. thinking for decades. This simple categorization into strategic and tactical may have as much to do with the dominance of nuclear weapons in military thinking about weapons utility generally as with any specific attributes of chemical or biological weapons. But these two scenarios no longer exhaust the subject.

(3) *Attacks on U.S. power projection forces:* Both chemical and biological weapons could come to be seen to be useful for attacking U.S. power projection forces in scenarios like that of the Persian Gulf war. A variety of scenarios merit consideration. Military forces engaged in active combat might well be subjected to attack by a state seeking to degrade U.S. abilities to prosecute a high intensity conflict over time. Military forces deployed in theater or offshore might be subject to attack prior to the outbreak of actual hostilities. Military forces en route to the theater, or at their points of embarkation or debarkation, might be similarly attacked in an effort to limit reinforcements or break logistic lines.

For each of these purposes, the ability to employ biological weapons in surreptitious fashion adds to their potential appeal. Use of a nuclear weapon for any of these purposes would likely invoke a prompt and overwhelming U.S. reaction, whereas the uncertainty attached to an outbreak of infectious disease for which no state claims responsibility would make the domestic and international politics of an overwhelming retaliation less easy to handle.

Variations on this scenario include the surreptitious introduction of biological weapons by a state not party to the conflict or by non-state actors seeking either to precipitate conflict or to bait an overreaction by the United States; such use would be aided by the fact that there is absence of a clear signature or clear attribution to the instigator of the attack.

This scenario may be increasingly probable if, as appears likely, leaders of states anticipating conflict with the United States or with a large international coalition learn the lessons of Iraq's mistake in allowing the coalition many months of buildup.

(4) *Escalation to chemical or biological weapons use in regional conflicts where the United States is not the primary target.* In this scenario U.S. forces would not be the intended target but would find themselves victims of an escalation to chemical or biological weapons by a state seeking to escalate a regional conflict (in which the United

States acts as a guarantor for one of the warring parties or perhaps for a regional neighbor). Illustrative examples include a North Korean attack on South Korea, Syrian attack on Israel, or Libyan attack on Egypt.

This scenario is increasingly likely given the proliferation of chemical and biological weapons in regions where the United States has security commitments or where the United Nations (UN) Security Council plays an important role, although important barriers remain related to the risks of retaliation by the attacked party or the United States.

(5) *Attack on U.S. targets in asymmetric strategies.* Asymmetric strategies are those pursued by weak states facing conflict with a strong state, whereby they seek to pit their strengths against the weaknesses of the stronger state. Such strategies are a subject of increasing discussion in the developing world in the wake of the Persian Gulf War. Biological weapons may have a special utility in these strategies. They are conceived as enabling weak authoritarian states to exploit their supposed strengths (such as freedom from the moral restriction against BW) while exploiting a perceived U.S. weakness (its supposed intolerance for high casualties and a political process that may be manipulable to produce a congressional veto of the use of force). The use of biological weapons in terrorist attacks on U.S. cities, in covert attacks on U.S. military depots, or in selective attacks on symbols of U.S. power might be attempted in the hope of inducing caution in the U.S. Congress, especially if the casualties were limited but more could plausibly be threatened. The purpose of BW attack in this scenario would not be decisive military advantage but the generation of public fear and its manipulation for political purposes. Biological weapons might have a special allure for these purposes given the greater plausible deniability of biological relative to nuclear attack. Such strategies may represent a fundamental misreading of the American temper and of the political effect of killing Americans, but this has not deprived them of their

currency in some countries contemplating war with the United States or a coalition led by it.

There is a particularly worrying vulnerability for U.S. allies in these scenarios. In conflicts where they figure as partners in a U.S.-led coalition, they may well be perceived as points of particular leverage on U.S. will. In a replay of the Persian Gulf War, selective and covert biological attacks by Iraq on European cities could be used to try to generate political pressure on the United States not to prosecute a war. They might also backfire, however, and deepen resolve to seek a prompt and decisive military solution to the problem.

This scenario is also rated increasingly likely as states contemplating a possible war with the United States study the Persian Gulf war for lessons.

(6) *Attack on economic targets.* One of the oldest uses of biological weapons is to destroy agricultural (both plants and livestock) or other environmental assets of economic value. With the ongoing boom in the application of biotechnology to agricultural purposes, it may well be that states will find it useful to exploit this technology to target the crops, livestock, or other natural economic assets of an adversary state, presumably surreptitiously. Is it far-fetched to think that in a future energy crisis U.S. corn crops might be targeted for destruction in an effort to further diminish U.S. energy self-reliance? Or that the U.S. cattle stock might be targeted in the wake of a major crop failure, to heighten economic instability in the United States?

A variation on this scenario would be the waging of biotechnology-based economic warfare by non-state actors, whether secessionist groups seeking indirectly to depopulate areas or criminal entities seeking to eliminate competitors.

This scenario is one that has received minimal consideration and is consequently rated fairly remote but also increasingly likely.

(7) *Retribution*: Chemical and biological weapons might come to be seen as useful for individuals, usually non-state actors, seeking to settle a grudge against the United States. This is a form of terrorism aimed not at securing a political concession from the United States or some other political or economic good but simply a humbling and weakening of the United States. Combine the motives of the Oklahoma City bombers with the technical sophistication of the Tokyo cult, and the result may well be superterrorism, i.e., terrorism aimed at inflicting unprecedented levels of casualties.

There are two variants of this scenario that deserve particular attention. One is attack on the United States for messianic purposes by individuals motivated by a worldview born of a particular value-laden orientation or ideology that views American values and society as anathema and an evil that must be purged from the globe. The other is less likely but not implausible: a coalition of international criminal groups in loose affiliation with one or two key disaffected states that might target a handful of U.S. cities for biological attack not so much for retribution as to try to eliminate the United States as a major power on the world scene.

Whether this scenario is growing more or less likely cannot be known. But it cannot be dismissed.

The cumulative picture that emerges from this survey is a disturbing one. The dominant way of thinking about chemical and biological weapons is revealed as biased, and dangerously so. That bias derives from an era, now past, when nuclear weapons dominated in U.S. strategic analysis. It also derives from a view of the technical features of chemical and biological weapons that is not current. A changing security environment and an evolving technology base compel a rethinking of the character and scale of the risks associated with the proliferation of chemical and biological weapons. They cannot be ignored. Nor can they be understood using ideas crafted for the nuclear or conventional domains. These weapons complicate our understanding of the emerging security requirement. Large risks exist, with larger risks on the horizon. But how profound or novel are the challenges these weapons pose? There are many steps that the United States—and its allies—can take to undermine the military value of such weapons in attack on the United States or U.S.-led coalitions. If these steps are carefully conceived and fully implemented, it is reasonable to conclude that the chemical and biological capabilities extant in the world today will not require a fundamental rethinking of the U.S. world role as an underwriter of security for others. The biological dimension in particular, however, stands out as requiring particular attention if this relatively sanguine conclusion is to stand the test of time.

Implications for Security Strategies

Do the vulnerabilities of U.S. forces and the U.S. populace to chemical and biological weapons matter? Risks, after all, are a standard part of the military equation. How are the factors enumerated above relevant for the security strategies of the United States? This section examines the implications of chemical and biological weapons proliferation for some basic elements of U.S. international security policy.

(1) *Challenges to power projection*: A cornerstone of U.S. security strategy after the Cold War is the projection of power into zones of conflict. The proliferation of chemical and biological weapons complicates this, in some ways significantly so. For purposes of this assessment, it is useful to distinguish between three types of power projection: to "show the flag" and demonstrate presence; to honor alliance relations with regional partners; and to intervene, whether collectively in support of a UN Security Council resolution or unilaterally in defense of regional interests.

The presence function is often accomplished with naval forces. But offshore operations are increasingly at risk with the proliferation of anti-ship cruise missiles and other advanced coastal policing assets;

chemical and in particular biological upwind attack cannot be ruled out. This risk is, of course, a function of the geography of specific regions as it is of the attributes of specific weapons. In the Persian Gulf, for example, Iranian anti-ship missiles increased the risks of the commercial vessel reflagging exercise of the late 1980s, and the Iranian naval buildup of the 1990s has greatly increased the risks to foreign naval vessels operating there. One possible response to the heightened missile threat is to depend increasingly on submarines for power projection, but by their very invisibility they are less well suited to the presence function of naval forces in "show the flag" operations.

The alliance function is usually accomplished with a mix of locally deployed forces and political commitments to extend protection in case of war or threatened war. At the very least, proliferation increases the risks to locally deployed forces while also increasing the difficulty of deploying reinforcements in time of war or near war. It also magnifies the challenge of reassuring allies in zones of conflict; some may conclude that their vulnerability to chemical and biological attack, particularly on cities, makes the cost of remaining a U.S. ally too high.

In a broader political sense, CBW proliferation is likely to be seen to raise the potential costs of exercising military functions in support of alliance commitments, thus casting further doubt on the credibility of extended deterrence. As the history of the transatlantic alliance well demonstrates, the credibility of such deterrence is often in doubt, whatever the facts may be. As one study of great powers in world politics has concluded, "at the moment of trial, when the friendly superpower is supposed to meet its commitment—not only to warn and deter, but to come to the small nation's aid—reluctance often outweighs commitment."[11] Especially in regions where the United States does not have a strong national interest other than credibility, such potential costs may be seen to reinforce its reluctance to use force and thus weaken its political role.

The intervention function is usually accomplished by the insertion of military forces into hostile settings, where they must fight to control the situation on the ground. As Fred Iklé and Albert Wohlstetter have observed,

> The arsenals of the lesser powers will make it riskier and more difficult for the superpowers to intervene in regional wars. The U.S. ability to support its allies around the world will increasingly be called into question. Where American intervention seems necessary, it will generally require far more cooperation with Third World countries than has been required in the past.[12]

Accustomed to thinking of conflict with regional adversaries in "low-intensity" terms, the intervening powers must now anticipate mid- and high-intensity operations, as the British learned in the Falklands/Malvinas conflict and as the international coalition learned in expelling Iraq from Kuwait.

In some states of the developing world open discussion of the need to create a deterrent to intervention by developed states can be found. The former Indian Army chief of staff, General K. Sundarji, has endorsed a "minimum deterrent" meant to discourage "U.S. bullying" and "possible racist aggression from the West."[13] Two other Indian analysts have pointed out that: "Sophisticated weapons can come in handy for inflicting punishing damage by a technologically superior nation on a less capable one. They also may be useful for developing nations to raise the cost of intervention and to help in defense, as detailed in *Discriminate Deterrence.*"[14] Muammar Qaddafi has called for "a deterrent—missiles that could reach New York. . . . We should build this force so that they and others will no longer think about an attack."[15]

Intervention scenarios also seem to increasingly require some form of international legitimization before they receive the support of the U.S. public and Congress. Sustaining coalitions in international organizations in favor of intervention in the face of chemical or biological threats may prove particularly challenging. The solidarity of the permanent members of the Security Council in a future enforcement action cannot be taken for granted when they are not equally vulnerable.

In sum, the proliferation of chemical and biological weapons, in conjunction with other advanced military capabilities, has made the projection of power more difficult and costly, and the proliferation of weapons of mass destruction in particular has increased the likelihood that the costs of projection in human terms could be large. This has accelerated the passing of an era in which the advanced powers of the developed world could intervene militarily in the developing one without serious military costs. As Les Aspin argued, in the past nuclear weapons "were the great equalizer that enabled Western capitals to deal with numerically larger Eastern bloc forces....Nuclear weapons still serve the same purpose—as a great equalizer. But it is the United States that is now the potential equalizee."[16] Biological weapons may also operate as such an equalizer of U.S. power.

The new vulnerabilities described here could have a domestic political impact as well that is relevant to the intervention question. As the U.S. public comes to understand the heightened risks associated with the projection of power abroad, or as those risks are magnified through relentless television coverage, public reluctance to support such deployments will probably increase.

(2) *Challenges to regional security strategies.* As often noted, U.S. security interests have become increasingly regional in orientation with the passing of the bipolar order. How does CBW proliferation influence the regional security strategies of the United States?

It is important to recall the potential impact of chemical weapons in the European theater. Those familiar with the effort to modernize the U.S. chemical retaliatory capability with binary weapons in the early 1980s will remember that congressional approval was achieved largely by the argument that the large, ongoing investment in conventional force modernization was held hostage to the Achilles' heel of the chemical imbalance. In a NATO-Warsaw Pact war, chemical weapons might well have made the difference between victory or defeat (biological weapons were given scant attention and thus their potential role in such a war was dangerously and largely ignored). In the contemporary security environment, does a similar possibility exist?

The closest possibility is in Northeast Asia, where North Korea is poised to use both chemical and biological weapons. The vulnerability of domestic populations in South Korea and elsewhere in the region to such attack is more pronounced than military vulnerability (although military vulnerability to biological attack cannot be dismissed). But there are few better examples of the relevance of strong and effective protective measures as a tool for diminishing the impact of potential North Korean attack with chemical or biological weapons. Given that U.S. strategy in Northeast Asia emphasizes overlapping bilateral and multilateral components, backed by a substantial U.S. presence, chemical and biological weapons might well be seen by North Korea as a way to weaken coalitions in time of war or prevent or forestall the deployment of additional U.S. forces.

The Middle East poses a different kind of challenge, one in which many of the parties to the Arab-Israeli and the Persian Gulf conflicts appear capable of waging war with unconventional weapons. In such a war, the United States might be either target or bystander, and vulnerable in either role. There is wide recognition in the region of the tangible military benefits that would have accrued to Iraq had Saddam Hussein opted to attack air and naval ports and other logistics nodes with chemical weapons. The U.S. strategy of active military engagement through naval presence, peacekeeping, and bilateral contacts presents targets for CBW-armed adversaries. In a region where there are significant doubts about the U.S. staying power and the credibility of its guarantees, proliferation further erodes U.S. standing. Moreover, the state-sponsored terrorism that erupts from this region is a reminder of the vulnerability of U.S. cities when basic questions of U.S. will are in question.

In Europe itself, chemical and biological weapons are not entirely irrelevant today. The conflict in Bosnia has generated many reports, particularly of chemical weapons use. Deployment of U.S. forces there may well result in U.S. chemical casualties—and public outcries either to withdraw or to retaliate.

In other regions, chemical and biological weapons are virtually irrelevant to the security dynamic. In Latin America, the core foundation is cooperative and comprehensive security, although the tradition of opposition to U.S. imperialism may yet produce non-state actors willing to use unconventional weapons to prevent U.S. military engagement regionally. In sub-Saharan Africa, interstate war involving chemical and biological weapons appears for now to be a remote possibility, although the public health and biomedical consequences of any U.S. deployment in the region cannot easily be ignored.

In general, the effect of CBW proliferation in these regions is to complicate the achievement of stable military balances and to create new challenges for the conduct of military operations above the conventional but below the nuclear level. Proliferation also heightens the risk of war in a number of ways. It nourishes the ambitions of regional hegemons, increases regional frictions and thus the number of military crises, decreases the ability to coerce states away from the brink of war, heightens the risk of unauthorized or accidental use of weapons of mass destruction, increases the incentive to shoot first in time of near war, increases the destructiveness of war when it occurs, and improves the ability of regional actors to threaten military conflict outside the region.

(3) *Challenges to the strategy of fighting wars on U.S. terms.* One of the central purposes of the counterproliferation initiative is to ensure the ability of the United States to fight wars on its terms,

rather than those of the adversary—to fight with the weapons of U.S. choice, at a time and place of U.S. choosing, for purposes and aims formulated in Washington. CBW proliferation poses challenges here as well.

In regions where chemical and biological weapons are conceived as interim steps in the escalation ladder (as arguably in Northeast Asia), such proliferation may make the step to nuclear use seem less dramatic. CBW proliferation makes it more difficult to keep local conflicts local as U.S. allies or others beyond a region are attacked—or when surreptitious attack is made on the United States or its allies. It makes compromise by the United States more likely, when the costs of sticking to preferred positions is made to look too high. If the United States were to acquire the reputation as a state that can be blackmailed, there would be repercussions well beyond regional battlefields.

Arguably, the perception of heightened risk and vulnerability may precipitate a decline in defense spending and a further narrowing of U.S. power projection capabilities, on the grounds that it is foolish to sustain readiness for wars that the United States would not choose to fight or would win only at high cost in terms of chemical or biological attacks on U.S. cities. Such a decline of spending and capabilities may not, however, diminish the public expectation that U.S. forces be ready to fight and prevail in those circumstances where compelling national interests require action.

In conclusion, military vulnerabilities in the chemical and biological domains (as in the nuclear) impinge increasingly on the national strategic choices confronting the United States in the post-Cold War era. As yet, those challenges are not profound, although they are perhaps underappreciated in the Middle East and East Asia. But the trends raise fundamental questions about the U.S. world role and the use of military power as a primary means of global engagement—and these are trends that will play out in a decade or two, not half a century.

Challenges to Planning Assumptions

The final section of this paper focuses on the challenges to the planning assumptions that underpin current U.S. military policy in the chemical and biological domains. Three invalid assumptions stand out.

The first incorrect assumption is that the problems created by chemical and biological weapons can be lumped into either the nuclear or the conventional domain as a matter of military planning. It is commonly argued that biological weapons should be treated like nuclear weapons, and that chemical weapons should be treated as an extension of the contact battle. This view puts the Army as lead agency, with only very limited interest on the part of the Air Force and Navy. It unhelpfully results in biological defense being disregarded as an apparently minor subset of the potential chemical and biological warfare threat spectrum. And worse, biological defense is regarded as a biomedical nuisance, relegated to the margins of concern. This view also reinforces reliance on conventional preponderance in dealing with battlefield challenges when such preponderance may not always be locally available. It slights substantial vulnerabilities to non-strategic biological attack and misreads the potential strategic applications of chemical weapons in regional conflicts.

The conventional, chemical, nuclear, and biological problems should be conceived as an overlapping set of concentric circles of increasing radius that reflect their differential potential to cause casualties. Their many shared similarities do not rule out important differences.

The second invalid assumption is that a bit more readiness in the area of chemical and biological self-protection will solve the problem. More readiness is essential—the large gap between requirements and performance by U.S. forces is an age-old theme in the commentaries of non-military and non-U.S. but allied observers. It was of course brought home forcefully by the military itself in the own assessment of the near-brush with Iraq's chemical and biological weapons in the Persian Gulf War.[17] But more readiness will not redress the challenges posed to battlefield tactics, theater operations, and national strategy. Moreover, perfect readiness is not possible.

The purposes of military planning should be to diminish the risk posed by such weapons in the hands of possible adversaries, raise the thresholds at which such weapons become militarily significant, and reduce the perception that the United States can be blackmailed through weaknesses in this area. As noted below, achievement of these aims will require an understanding within the U.S. military of the ways in which its programs and policies must be complementary to and integrated with other instruments of U.S. policy aimed at limiting or eliminating such threats and a stronger appreciation of its role in making the chemical and biological arms control regimes function effectively, akin to its now well understood role in the nuclear and conventional domains.

The third incorrect assumption is that there are straightforward means to deter the use of chemical and biological weapons. Indeed, existing thinking about the deterrence of chemical and biological attack on the United States or its forces is shown to be threadbare the further one probes into the subject.

During the Cold War, the United States had a set of policies for deterring the use of chemical and biological weapons suited to the time. In the chemical domain, it relied on an in-kind retaliatory capability to deter the use of such weapons in an East-West confrontation. The deterrent effect was believed to derive from the ability to deny the Warsaw Pact control of a heavily armored and fast-paced conventional battlefield through the selective and one-sided use of such weapons, by imposing upon Pact forces the onerous effects of fighting at all times in a chemically protected posture, not just at times and places of their choosing. The belief that such deterrence might work was reinforced by historical experience: no nation possessing chemical weapons has been attacked with chemical weapons by another state. It should be noted that this historical experience is rather limited and the lessons selectively drawn. Additional deterrence benefits in the chemical domain derive from the protective capacities of U.S. forces—their ability to sustain combat on a contaminated battlefield through the use of individual and collective protection systems.

With the passing of the Cold War and in an effort to accelerate conclusion of the Chemical Weapons Convention, the United States in 1991 relinquished its right to retaliation in kind and committed itself to destroying its chemical weapons stockpile. The decision was based in part on the view that in the post-Cold War era the United States is unlikely to face an ally capable of using chemical weapons in the way that the Warsaw Pact could, to immobilize and defeat U.S. forces, or whose military operations could be degraded in some unique way by U.S. chemical retaliation as opposed to other forms of escalation or punishment. This view was reinforced by a belief that greater military benefits were to be derived from the CWC in the form of deterrence of CW programs in countries of concern and a minimizing of the strategic impact of any remaining programs by keeping them small and technically underdeveloped.

In the biological domain, a different history of deterrence can be traced to 1969. First, with unilateral biological disarmament at that time, the United States no longer relies on in-kind deterrence and relies instead on conventional preponderance and the threat of nuclear escalation to deter biological attack on U.S. targets. Second, it pursues a research and development program aimed solely at defensive measures, including vaccine production, other forms of prophylactic and protective measures, and diagnostic capabilities. These are pursued on an open basis in order not to generate fears that the United States is covertly producing new BW agents for offensive purposes.

Given the passing of the Cold War and with it the easy reliance of the United States on nuclear weapons, it is logical to ask whether the United States can continue to dismiss the potential value of an in-kind BW deterrent. The question is logical but the answer is unchanged. Any attempt by the United States to recreate a stockpile of biological weapons would probably precipitate a broad international movement toward the production of biological weapons, thus greatly magnifying the problem that the step was intended to redress. But it is also clear that the ready recourse to nuclear retaliation cannot be taken for granted in the post-Cold War world and that U.S. policymakers cannot continue to avoid the BW problem as an issue of strategic policy. It is also clear that in conflicts such as the Persian Gulf war there are means of escalation other than those derived from the use of more potent weapons, such as the expansion of war aims (e.g., beyond expulsion of Iraqi forces from Kuwait to control of Iraq and removal of the ruling regime).

When faced with a decision about how to respond to a specific instance of biological (and chemical) attack, U.S. commanders will have to assess first whether any specific departure from existing strategy is called for. Biological attack in desperation may result in a militarily irrelevant impact and, if significant casualties have not resulted, the only necessary U.S. response may be a political one. But biological attack that significantly degrades U.S. operations might well be met with escalation of the conflict by conventional means or by an expansion of war aims. In cases where such attack cripples U.S. military operations and threatens defeat of U.S. forces, command authorities will likely consider escalation to nuclear use. Biological attack on U.S. population centers, or those of its allies, will involve a similar but not identical set of retaliatory questions related to public attitudes and expectations of the political result of a retaliatory strike. It is important to note, however, that the United States has forsworn certain retaliatory options in the context of the Nuclear Non-Proliferation Treaty (NPT); specifically, it has made a binding negative security assurance not to use nuclear weapons to attack a non-nuclear weapon state, without reference to the latter's possible use of chemical or biological weapons. However useful this may have been for extending the NPT, it has had little-contemplated consequences for the deterrence of strategic biological attack.

The United States will thus continue to rely on its defensive CBW capacities to deter and defeat CBW attack. In fact, major improvement in these capacities will reap large deterrence benefits. Glaring deficiencies were brought into the open by the Persian Gulf War. The Counterproliferation Initiative establishes a high priority for redressing shortcomings in the ability of U.S. military forces to operate successfully on a battlefield contaminated by chemical weapons and involving an airborne biological threat.

For the BW problem, the following specific priorities stand out: (1) an improved ability to detect and map the battlefield BW hazard, currently rudimentary at best; (2) an improved protective kit for individual soldiers that would drop reliance on the chemical protective gear when less onerous masks alone are sufficient for meeting virtually all BW threats (and skin coverage is virtually unnecessary); (3) immediate availability of vaccines for BW agents known to be deployed (the Persian Gulf War revealed the absence of vaccines in sufficient quantities for even the standard anthrax threat); (4) stronger abilities to identify, diagnose, and provide medical counters for soldiers and populations attacked with biological weapons; (5) theater missile defenses capable of defeating not just ballistic but also cruise missiles (the latter far superior delivery vehicles for biological agents and themselves proliferating in large numbers) and in a way that does so at sufficient height and sufficient lethality to destroy all submunitions and so prevent downwind hazards; (5) improved decontamination capabilities, especially for naval and air forces; and (6) a vaccines program not limited to measures solely against standard agents well known by the 1960s.

A more comprehensive program of CBW defense and continued emphasis on preponderant conventional forces should prove significant and reliable counters to the traditional uses of CBW discussed above. But what about the non-traditional uses, particularly of biological agents?

For scenarios involving non-traditional uses, deterrence-based strategies focused specifically on BW concerns would appear to have little or no utility. U.S. policy in these cases must be aimed not at preventing biological attack but preventing attack generally. This is a wider task of policy beyond the scope of BW defense but it has BW defense implications. For meeting these contingencies the United States needs strong response capabilities, especially diagnostic ones (to diminish the plausible deniability factor) and medical treatment ones (to limit outbreaks and treat the ill) for large public outbreaks. Currently, U.S. capabilities are scaled to outbreaks that are natural rather than man-made and would likely be overwhelmed by the unconventional, covert use of infectious materials in attacking the U.S. population or agricultural resources.

This analysis points to two further tasks of U.S. policy. One is endeavoring to ensure that the CBW problem remains essentially at its present scale and does not grow orders of magnitude worse. For this purpose, providing U.S. leadership to the existing international control regimes in this area is an important prerequisite. The Chemical Weapons Convention and the Biological and Toxin Weapons Convention are both imperfect treaties; despite much disarmament rhetoric, neither will eliminate the weapons of concern. But their utility for the task described above should not be slighted. By keeping the number of chemical and biological weapons arsenals few, by keeping their size limited, and by making technical advance difficult, they can play a valuable role in minimizing the security challenges to the United States posed by weapons programs of proliferation concern. Strengthening these regimes and deterring potential proliferators also requires success in the effort to control Iraq's unconventional weapons programs and to deal with other compliance problems, such as concerns about Russia's lingering BW program.

The other task is to endeavor to ensure that the United States does not emerge as a target of individuals or states motivated by a resentment of U.S. power. For this purpose, attending to the perceived legitimacy of the basic institutions of global governance and of U.S. preeminence in its unipolar moment is essential. If the United States comes to be seen as the primary defender of an outdated and unjust world system in which major international institutions and U.S. power are used to defend the privileges of the prosperous and secure with little attention to the needs or ambitions of states and peoples aspiring to a large world role, a global division may emerge between states desirous of change and status quo powers. Such a conflict, and the perceptions that fuel it, could lead to the most worrisome of the BW scenarios.

Without success at these two tasks, the BW problem may well worsen to the point that it is not amenable to traditional military strategies of deterrence and defense. The U.S. military is not at the forefront of either of these tasks but it can lend weight and encouragement to debate within the security policy community about their urgency.

Conclusion

The near brush with Iraq's chemical and biological weapons in 1991 usefully shook the complacency that has long gripped much of the military community in thinking about the chemical and biological subject. But lingering tension between complacency and panic has delayed a clear focus on the problem.

Much of the conceptual baggage of the past must be set aside as technically ill-informed and strategically time-bound. The steady accretion of chemical and biological war-fighting capabilities in regions of key strategic interest to the United States cannot be understood or responded to with old approaches. Such proliferation must be understood as touching on a broad array of U.S. military, political, and strategic interests. Neither today nor in the near-term future does such proliferation promise a fundamental reorientation of regional or global affairs. But the problem is not a static one, and failure to take steps to shape its future evolution now could result in a world in which the use of U.S. military power is virtually vetoed by even the smallest country. Understanding the ways in which the risks of chemical and biological weapons are different from conventional wisdoms about them is the point of departure for more effective policy.

Notes

1. Testimony by the director of U.S. naval intelligence, Rear Admiral Thomas A. Brooks, to the Subcommittee on Seapower, Strategic, and Critical Materials of the House Armed Services Committee, March 7, 1991. See also U.S. Congress, House of Representatives, Committee on Armed Services, *Countering the Chemical and Biological Weapons Threat in the Post-Soviet World*, Report of the Special Inquiry into the Chemical and Biological Threat, February 23, 1993 (Washington, D.C.: GPO, 1993).

2. See "Implications of Soviet Use of Chemical and Toxin Weapons for U.S. Security Interests," *Chemical and Engineering News*, February 25, 1985, about a leaked U.S. national intelligence estimate.

3. Brooks testimony of March 7, 1991.

4. Testimony of William F. Burns, then director of the U.S. Arms Control and Disarmament Agency, as reported in "Agency Gets Last Word on Poison Gas," *Washington Post*, December 13, 1989. The article discusses administration attempts to revise Burns's testimony after his departure from government on this specific point.

5. For a critical evaluation of the tendency to overstate the nature and character of chemical weapons proliferation, see Julian Perry Robinson, "Chemical Weapons Proliferation: The Problem in Perspective," in Trevor Findlay, ed., *Chemical Weapons and Missile Proliferation: With Implications for the Asia/Pacific Region* (Boulder, Colo.: Lynne Rienner Publishers, 1991), pp. 19-35.

6. See "New Challenges and New Policy Priorities for the 1990s," in Roberts, ed., *Biological Weapons: Weapons of the Future?* (Washington, D.C.: Center for Strategic and International Studies, 1993), especially pp. 74-75. See also in that volume W. Seth Carus, "The Proliferation of

Biological Weapons," and Graham Pearson, "Biological Weapons: The British View," as well as "Eleven Countries `Defying Ban on Germ Weapons'," *The Guardian*, November 5, 1991, p. 1.

7. For a review of these allegations by the U.S. government, see Elisa D. Harris, Statement to the Defense, Foreign Policy, and Space Task Force of the Budget Committee of the U.S. House of Representatives, May 22, 1991. A report of the Foreign Intelligence Service of Russia released in February 1993 provided a comprehensive assessment of the unconventional weapons capabilities, and an unprecedented level of detail about alleged biological weapons programs, in the developing world. See "A New Challenge After the Cold War: The Proliferation of Weapons of Mass Destruction," a report prepared by the Foreign Intelligence Service of the Russian Federation (Moscow, 1993), translated by Foreign Broadcast Information Service in February 1993. Summary and excerpts made available by U.S. Committee on Government Affairs, U.S. Senate, February 24, 1993, and subsequently published in *Proliferation Threats of the 1990's*, Hearing Before the Committee on Governmental Affairs, U.S. Senate, 103rd Cong., 1st Sess., February 24, 1993 (Washington, D.C.: GPO, 1993).

8. See testimony by then director of central intelligence, William Webster, of February 9, 1989, in *Global Spread of Chemical and Biological Weapons*, Hearings Before the Committee on Governmental Affairs and Its Permanent Subcommittee on Investigations, U.S. Senate, February 9-10, May 2, 17, 1989 (Washington, D.C.: GPO, 1989).

9. See "General Quizzed on Chemical Weapons Production," *Izvestiia*, in Foreign Broadcast Information Service—Soviet Union-92-082, April 28, 1992.

10. See Carus, "The Proliferation of Biological Weapons." See also "Iraqi CBW Armament and the UN Special Commission," *Chemical Weapons Convention Bulletin*, No. 13 (September 1991), pp. 21-22.

11. Yohanan Cohen, *Small Nations in Times of Crisis and Confrontation* (New York, N.Y.: State University of New York Press, 1989), pp. 338-339.

12. Commission on Integrated Long-Term Strategy, *Discriminate Deterrence* (Washington, D.C.: GPO, January 1988), p. 10.

13. Foreign Broadcast Information Service, *Daily Report: Near East and South Asia* (FBIS-NES-92-199), October 14, 1992, p. 46.

14. C. Raja Mohan and K. Subrahmanyam, "High-Technology Weapons in the Developing World," in Eric Arnett, ed., *Science and Security:*

Technology Advances and the Arms Control Agenda (Washington, D.C.: American Association for the Advancement of Science, 1989), p. 236.

15. Speech by Muammar Qaddafi at a meeting of students of the Higher Institute for Applied Social Studies at the Great al-Fatih University, April 18, 1990, translated in FBIS-NES-90-078, April 23, 1990, p. 8.

16. Les Aspin, *From Deterring to Denuking: Dealing with Proliferation in the 1990s* (Washington, D.C.: House Committee on Armed Services, 1992), p. 4.

17. See *Conduct of the Persian Gulf War: Final Report to Congress* (Washington, D.C.: Department of Defense, April 1992). See also Les Aspin and William Dickinson, *Defense for a New Era: Lessons of the Persian Gulf War* (Washington, D.C.: Brassey's, 1992).

✦ Deterrence and Warfighting in an NBC Environment

JEROME H. KAHAN

U. S. forces face many challenges in the post-Cold War world, but none may demand newer and more different ways of planning and executing military operations than dealing with regional adversaries who possess arsenals of nuclear, biological, or chemical (NBC) weapons. In the near to mid-term, approximately two dozen regional states could acquire militarily-usable NBC weapons. With the exception of Israel, these NBC proliferants are not friendly toward the United States. Of particular concern is the fact that Iran, Iraq, and North Korea could confront the United States with all three types of NBC threats. Over the longer run, dozens of additional nations could develop NBC capabilities. Sophisticated means of delivery are also becoming available, including cruise as well as ballistic missiles and advanced aircraft.[1]

Mr. Kahan is Director of Regional Issues at the Center for Naval Analyses (CNA). The opinions expressed in this paper are those of the author, and do not necessarily represent those of CNA, the Department of the Navy, or the Department of Defense.

NBC weapons employed against our forces and bases would at the very least create complications in the conduct of any military campaign. Depending upon the size, scope, and character of NBC use, the consequences could be devastating, with great loss of life and possible alterations in U.S. war aims. "Business as usual" for our military forces is not an appropriate response. Regional NBC threats pose challenges that differ in kind, not simply in degree, from earlier Cold War challenges and the conventional contingencies currently driving our force planning and defense posture.

This paper investigates three questions that must be addressed by U.S. military planners in preparing to deal with regional NBC threats:[2]

• How can we deter NBC use against forward-based U.S forces or forces deploying overseas to respond to contingencies?
• What countermeasures are available to protect U.S. forces against NBC attacks, minimize their exposure, and enable them to accomplish their mission?
• What plans, policies, and preparations should be pursued to place U S. forces in a better position to deter NBC threats and operate in an NBC environment?

Principles of Deterrence

If our national interests were endangered, the United States might decide to intervene militarily in a regional conflict in which an adversary had NBC weapons. But many small states acquire NBC weapons precisely to prevent U.S. intervention by raising the costs and risks of such an action. Accordingly, a fundamental U.S. national objective is to avoid "self-deterrence"—that is, a reluctance to commit our forces to deal with an important crisis or conflict because the adversary is armed with NBC weapons.[3]

While deterrence of *initial use* is crucial, once the NBC threshold is crossed the United States will still need to deter *further use* of whatever type of NBC weapon was employed (e.g., chemical) as well as escalation to other types of available NBC weapons (e.g., nuclear or biological). Without an effective approach to what can be termed as "intrawar NBC deterrence," U.S. forces will risk being exposed to a continuing barrage of NBC strikes.

Elements of Deterrence

Deterrence of NBC use by regional adversaries against U.S. forces—whether initially or to thwart continuing employment—can be brought about in one of two ways or a combination of both.[4]

Threat of Retaliation. Deterrence can be accomplished if the NBC-armed adversary is convinced that NBC use against U.S. forces will lead to military retaliation with consequences to the prospective perpetrator that far outweigh the anticipated gains and benefits.

Denial of Success. Deterrence can also be accomplished if the prospective perpetrator believes that use of NBC weapons against U.S. forces will not stop our campaign or cause us to disengage due to physical damage, psychological impact, or political concerns.[5]

Retaliatory threats need to be credible to an adversary contemplating NBC strikes against U.S. forces. Our resolve would need to be conveyed through public and private statements, and our force posture would have to be seen as capable of carrying out effective retaliatory actions. Within the U.S. Government, we would require procedures that allow timely decisions on whether, when, and how to retaliate against NBC use.

However, it would not be prudent to rely entirely on deterrence through the threat of retaliation. Countermeasures should be taken to deny the adversary success in employing NBC weapons by limiting damage to our forces, reducing their exposure, and retaining their military effectiveness and psychological will. These countermeasures cannot only contribute to deterrence, but can also enable U.S. forces to operate in an NBC environment if deterrence fails.

The Threat of Retaliation[6]

No fixed rules exist for implementing a retaliatory policy in response to NBC use under all circumstances. For example, very limited chemical weapons attacks against U.S. forces with minimal casualties may not warrant a special form of retaliation. On the other hand, widespread and effective use of nuclear weapons or biological agents causing thousands of fatalities might well justify a nuclear response. A sensible approach should take into account the proportionality of any response to the damage caused by NBC attacks as well as the need to show through retaliation that a fundamental principle is at stake when any nation crosses the threshold of NBC use. Further complicating this problem is the uncertainty over whether NBC-armed adversaries will perceive, understand, and be influenced by our retaliatory policy. In threatening NBC use, or in employing these weapons to achieve military or political aims, a regional state may have extremely strong national interests to further and protect. Leaders of these countries may be willing to take risks to achieve their goals that U.S. leaders might be unwilling to take. This does not necessarily mean that the foreign leaders are irrational; it may only mean that they have different goals and values than we do, and may weight costs and gains differently. These leaders may be willing to risk retaliation against their country, if they and their regime can survive. They may also be willing to use NBC weapons in desperation if their regime is threatened, even if this brings self-destruction.

How to Retaliate

In developing a retaliatory policy to deter NBC use against U.S. forces, we would have to decide what targets to retaliate against and whether to use conventional or nuclear weapons, since chemical and biological weapons options would not be available.[7] Underpinning these decisions is the fundamental question of the purpose to be served by responding to NBC use.   Three broad objectives for U.S. retaliation can be identified: destroying any residual NBC weapons to limit further damage; defeating the aggressor militarily by attacking all military targets; and punishing the perpetrator by retaliating in a substantial manner against the nation's infrastructure and possibly urban-industrial centers.

U.S. conventional weapons might be able to accomplish all these objectives with varying degrees of effectiveness.   In theory, launching disabling strikes in retaliation against an opponent's smaller and presumably disorganized remaining NBC sites would be easier than destroying a larger and battle-ready initial force.   But difficulties could still arise, particularly if the residual force is the best-protected component.   More feasible would be launching major conventional air strikes against a perpetrator's overall military establishment along the lines of the bombing campaign against Iraq in Desert Storm. Conducting devastating attacks against a set of crucial industrial, communications, and other infrastructure targets would also seem possible, especially given the nature of the regional states in question.

If the United States decides to use nuclear weapons in response to chemical or biological weapons attacks, this would put us in the position of *using nuclear weapons first* in a conflict.   On political grounds alone, it would be extremely difficult for a U.S. President to make such a decision.[8]   Even if an aggressor had used nuclear weapons against our forces, the broader question of whether we, as a superpower, should respond in kind to nuclear use is extremely controversial.   The military pros and cons of nuclear retaliation can be put forward by defense planners—balancing the need to strike back with devastating power against the collateral damage associated with nuclear attacks.   But again the issues of principle and proportionality arise, with military factors becoming quickly overshadowed by moral as well as political considerations.   A U.S. nuclear response would certainly send a strong message, but might not be judged by domestic and world opinion as proper or justified. And it is impossible to prove whether a U.S. nuclear response would have the effect of inhibiting other regional states from using NBC weapons or the opposite effect of persuading potential proliferants that these weapons are legitimate instruments of war.

Declaratory Policy

Existing U.S. policy on response to NBC use is somewhat ambiguous. This is not surprising, given the previous discussion of whether and how retaliation might be conducted. We have certainly made it known that we would view nuclear use against U.S. forces as an egregious act warranting a serious response, including the very real possibility of retaliation in kind.[9] We have also never ruled out the option of using nuclear weapons in response to chemical or biological attacks that endanger our interests.[10]

Greater precision attached to our retaliatory policy could enhance credibility and strengthen deterrence of NBC use. Too much uncertainty can backfire if an opponent underestimates our capacity and resolve or misreads ambiguity as a sign of weakness and a reluctance to retaliate. But too much specificity would reduce flexibility and possibly commit us to actions we may not wish to take. Indeed, U.S. leaders might not know in advance what actions they themselves would take in specific cases of impending or actual NBC use against U.S. military forces.

It is therefore important to balance ambiguity and precision in fashioning an official U.S. declaratory policy on response to the use of NBC weapons. Present U.S. policy on response to *nuclear use*, as articulated above, seems to represent a credible and balanced formulation. What is needed, however, is a declaratory policy dealing with response to *biological or chemical weapons use*, since it can be argued that U.S. forces are more likely to be threatened by these weapons in a battlefield context.[11] Here is a proposed formulation of a BW/CW declaratory policy, covering attacks against our military forces as well as other targets, that may meet this need:[12]

The U. S. regards the use of biological or chemical weapons as an unacceptable act. We will respond decisively to any use of such weapons and will take all appropriate actions to protect U.S. interests, including U.S. forces, citizens, and territories, from attack by biological or chemical weapons. The U.S. will support our allies and friendly states in such circumstances. The U.S. response to any chemical or biological attack will be overwhelming and will result in the gravest consequences.

Force Posturing

The movement or posturing of U.S. military forces can complement our declaratory statements, while at the same time positioning our forces to conduct retaliatory strikes if called upon to do so. U.S. military forces are the most powerful in the world, and any regional state contemplating use of NBC weapons must face the risk that this power will be used against them. During an impending crisis, we can send signals to regional NBC adversaries by increasing military readiness and placing certain forces on alert. If we wanted to underscore our commitment and capabilities to apply military force in deterring NBC use, we could announce and conduct specialized counterproliferation military exercises in or near regions of concern. Moving beyond exercises, we can also surge offensive and defensive forces forward to the region where NBC weapons are likely to be useddeploying naval task forces near the coast, tactical air forces to bases in the region, and Army units to overseas facilities.

Posturing our conventional forces alone might not send a sufficiently meaningful message to a prospective NBC aggressor. We might consider punctuating our policy by manipulating our strategic nuclear forces as well. But it is not clear that threats to use our most powerful forces will be as credible to small states as they presumably were to the former USSR. Moreover, regional states may not be able to detect and understand the significance of such strategic actions as opening ICBM silos or putting more SLBMs to sea. On the other hand, bomber movements to forward staging bases might be more easily detected, and overflights of these systems would not go unnoticed.

It is worth considering whether redeployment of Theater Nuclear Forces (TNF) on aircraft carriers, surface ships, and tactical aircraft would be effective in deterring regional NBC use. Deployment of TNF to regions of proliferation concern might more directly demonstrate our determination and have greater visibility and credibility than signalling with our intercontinental missiles and strategic bombers.

Countermeasures Against NBC Attack

As suggested, if the United States wants to avoid sole reliance on the threat of retaliation to deter NBC attacks, a series of additional countermeasures should be taken. These can be thought of as a multi-tiered series of steps which provide complementary and cascading capabilities. Each individual measure does not have to be 100 percent effective, as long as the elements as a whole strengthen deterrence and afford protection to U.S. forces if they are exposed to attack. The more important NBC countermeasures include counterforce strikes, active defenses, passive defenses, and specialized doctrine and training. Their purposes and problems, and how they interact, are discussed below.

In assessing the relative utility of NBC countermeasures, it is important to bear in mind that the military effectiveness of NBC weapons, especially in the hands of regional states, varies widely as a function of whether nuclear, biological, or chemical weapons are employed; what types of targets are attacked; how many weapons are launched; and what climatic conditions exist. Accordingly, both the need for and the efficacy of protective measures against NBC attacks will also vary. It is neither accurate nor helpful to refer to all NBC capabilities as representing a common category of "weapons of mass destruction."[13]

It is also important to recognize that conducting effective military operations against *combined* NBC threats poses particularly challenging problems for U.S. forces. Countermeasures against each type of threat are not necessarily congruent or synergistic. Different and potentially contending tactical decisions may have to be made by commanders on the scene who are uncertain over what forms of NBC attack might take place. A clever NBC-armed opponent can keep U.S. forces off-balance and in a non-optimum posture.

Counterforce Strikes

The United States could attempt to destroy or degrade an opponent's NBC weapons through military strikes, either before these weapons are employed or during an NBC campaign. Such offensive actions would physically prevent an NBC-armed state from launching its weapons or at least limit the amount of damage that could be inflicted on our forces. NBC-armed states might be dissuaded from even threatening to use their NBC weapons if they believed the U.S. had the capacity to launch disabling strikes. Once NBC weapons were used, we could employ counterforce attacks to contain further damage and help deter continued or expanded NBC attacks.

A comprehensive counterforce strike entails attacking all known NBC weapons and associated delivery systems in an opponent's country, both on-line and backup. Depending on geography, base availability, and the size and sophistication of the target set, the United States could use a wide range of systems to conduct these attacksconventionally armed strategic bombers, land- and sea-based tactical aircraft, and cruise missiles. Weapons with precision strike features, including terminal guidance, would be most effective, especially if connected to rapid damage assessment capabilities.

Conventional weapons would be preferable for this mission. As discussed above, whatever their military utility, it would be politically difficult for the United States to justify striking first with nuclear weapons to prevent a smaller state from using its chemical, biological, or even nuclear weapons. If NBC weapons are actually employed against our forces with devastating effect, the likelihood of the U.S. using nuclear weapons in counterforce strikes against residual NBC arsenals would increase.

In theory, the best defense might be to launch offensive attacks against an opponent's NBC arsenal early in a crisis. As a practical matter, however, execution of a counterforce strike is both technically demanding and politically controversial for a number of reasons:

- Unless we faced an extremely small and unsophisticated force in a country where our intelligence was superb, we would almost surely not be able to identify and locate all NBC targets. For example, NBC-armed missiles deployed on mobile launchers or hidden in caves would be difficult to discover.[14]
- Even if all targets were known to U.S intelligence, it would be almost impossible to destroy *all* of them *simultaneously*. Failure to fully and effectively accomplish this mission could result in the aggressor launching NBC weapons while under attack or retaining sufficient capabilities after a U.S. strike to retaliate against U.S. forces.
- Attacks on NBC sites could lead to the release of fissionable material, biological agents, or chemical contaminants, thereby causing collateral damage to civilian populations. This risk would place political inhibitions on U.S. leaders contemplating such a step.
- U.S. leaders would for political reasons tend to avoid authorizing counterforce strikes "out-of-the-blue." If a conventional conflict had begun, attacking enemy NBC sites would be more of a justified military action.

It is also possible for U.S. special forces to play a "counterforce" role in negating NBC threats by inserting themselves clandestinely in enemy territory, finding all the NBC weapons, providing targeting information for external strikes, and potentially capturing or permanently disarming NBC arsenals. However, the chances of successfully accomplishing such missions are extremely low, and it may not be worth the risk of U.S. forces being discovered and captured.

Active Defense

Active defenses encompass the full range of air and missile defenses—from defenses of ports, bases, and ground units, to medium- and long-range interceptors for destroying incoming aircraft, cruise missiles, and ballistic missiles. By potentially negating the ability of regional states to deliver NBC weapons on target, active defenses can dissuade an aggressor from using or threatening to use these weapons against U.S. forces. If these weapons are nonetheless employed, active defenses can prevent or at least limit damage to our forces. If U.S. counterforce strikes have been conducted with even modest success, our U.S. active defenses will have an easier task contending with attacks from residual NBC arsenals which are likely to be ragged and uncoordinated. A potential "virtual" benefit of the sheer presence of active defenses might be to cause an NBC-armed adversary to avoid attacking protected forces or areas, resulting in de-optimized strikes against less significant targets with corresponding reduced damage to U.S. forces.

While active defenses can in principle provide deterrence and damage-limiting payoffs in the face of regional NBC aggression, there are two practical limitations which restrict their utility as a countermeasure: availability and effectiveness.

Availability of Balanced Defenses

U.S. defenses against modern aircraft are available and relatively effective through a combination of fighter interceptors and both land- and sea-based surface-to-air missile systems. These air-defense systems also provide capabilities for intercepting cruise missiles, although their effectiveness against low-flying, low observable, and "smart" cruise missiles is open to question.

But whatever the effectiveness of U.S. defenses against air-breathing threats, we will not have a "balanced" active defense system in the near-term.[15] The gap in our arsenal centers around defenses against theater ballistic missiles.

U.S. Theater Missile Defense (TMD) programs available between now and the year 2000—consisting of land-based Patriot upgrades (PAC-3) and small numbers of sea-based Aegis lower-tier systems (SM-2 Block IV) will primarily provide limited protection for point targets. These systems can be useful, however, in defending ports and airfields against short-range ballistic missiles such as SCUD. Despite their small "footprints" and technical limitations, deployment of these systems can pose a "psychological deterrent" to an NBC-armed adversary. But neither Patriot nor lower-tier Aegis can contend with longer-range, more sophisticate theater ballistic threats represented by the Agni or Nodong missiles.[16]

More effective wide-area capabilities—represented by the land-based THAAD and upper-tier sea-based TMD systems—will not be available in meaningful numbers until after the year 2000 and probably no sooner than the year 2005.[17] Once available, these systems will be capable of engaging longer-range threats early in their launch trajectory, thus providing coverage for U.S. forces and facilities spread over a relatively wide area. Both systems could offer protection to U.S. forces and associated lines of supply as they moved away from coastal positions to fight in the interior.

Availability of active defense systems in the U.S. inventory is not the same as availability in theater to protect U.S. forces facing NBC threats. Depending upon the speed at which a crisis unfolds, U.S. defenses not already forward-based would have to be deployed to the region to cover existing forces and mate with arriving forces. While sea-based defensive systems might be able to arrive within the first few days, reinforcing land-based defenses may take substantially longer. U.S. forces could therefore be exposed to NBC attacks during the crucial early stages of a conflict.

Effectiveness against NBC Attack.

The performance requirements for defensive systems seeking to destroy NBC-armed aircraft or missiles are significantly greater than when facing conventional threats. Military forces do not expect active defenses to destroy the bulk of incoming attackers carrying conventional weapons. Attrition over time is the objective, with offensive forces taking conventional "hits" and carrying on their campaign.

But the NBC environment is different. Even a few nuclear bombs or missile warheads landing on or near military targets can cause devastating damage. One or two successful dispersions of biological agents by penetrating aircraft can wreak havoc. Although potentially less serious, small numbers of chemical rounds missed by defenses could create problems for U.S. forces conducting military operations.

To be sure, regional states may well present to U.S. defenses small numbers of relatively unsophisticated attacking aircraft or missiles armed with primitive NBC weapons. In this case, U.S. defenses might be capable of destroying virtually all incoming targets.

On the other hand, if an adversary launches large numbers of delivery systems carrying only small numbers of NBC weapons, U.S. defenses would not easily be able to differentiate between conventionally and non-conventionally armed attackers. This could lead to a high "leakage rate," possibly involving NBC penetration. It is also possible that U.S. defenses would run out of interceptors, thus giving remaining NBC weapons in the hand of an adversary a "free ride" to target.

Due to the twin problems of delayed availability and uncertain effectiveness, active defenses, notably TMD, will play only a restricted role as an NBC countermeasure for U.S. military forces in the near-term. Looking a decade or more ahead, however, the potential for active defenses to contribute to NBC deterrence and damage limitation will grow. The challenge to be overcome is for U.S. defensive technology and capabilities to keep ahead of the accelerating spread of NBC weapons and advanced delivery systems.[18]

Passive Defenses

While *active* defenses are designed to destroy systems carrying NBC weapons *before* they hit their targets, *passive* defenses are aimed at eliminating or mitigating the direct and indirect effects of NBC weapons that are *actually delivered* against U.S. forces.[19] The more an enemy's NBC arsenal is degraded by a combination of counterforce strikes and active defenses, the less demanding will be the need for passive defenses.

More than any other class of countermeasures, passive defenses are highly sensitive to the size and character of an NBC attack and the potential effectiveness of each type of weapon. Measures tailored to one specific form of NBC threat are not necessarily applicable to others. Accordingly, the following discussion deals separately with countermeasures against nuclear, biological, and chemical attacks.

Nuclear Weapons

Nuclear weapons are the most powerful means of inflicting serious damage on U.S. military personnel, bases, and equipment. Even if only a few nuclear weapons explode on or near massed military forces, they can have enormously destructive consequences that will occur immediately (blast and prompt radiation damage) and persist for long periods (fallout and long-term radiation damage.) These weapons are particularly threatening to concentrations of military force, such as support or depot facilities, ground troop formations, massed forces of tanks and other armored vehicles, and tightly clustered naval groups operating in littoral waters.

Passive defenses such as "hardening" equipment and communications against blasts or EMP can alleviate nuclear weapons effects. But these are costly steps that can encumber conventional operations without high confidence of success. On the other hand, providing forces with radiation detection devices, decontamination equipment, and medical treatment procedures are prudent steps worth taking, if both costs and expectations of benefits can be kept under control.

At the end of the day, physical protection of U.S. forces against nuclear attacks is simply not practicable. Reliance needs to placed on deterring nuclear strikes or destroying enemy arsenals on the ground or in flight. One mitigating consideration is the prospect that new nuclear states are likely to acquire in the near to mid-term relatively small nuclear arsenals (i.e., a few to a few dozen) with relatively low yields (i.e., tens rather than hundreds of kilotons). Regional states may also have difficulty delivering nuclear weapons to achieve maximum destructive impact. But small arsenals can still inflict significant damage, and, over time, even regional states can improve the size and sophistication of their nuclear arsenals, including delivery systems.

Biological Weapons

The effects of biological weapons are on personnel, not on equipment or property. In theory, if biological agents, lethal or non-lethal, were disseminated upwind near massed ground forces or airfields, they could cause serious damage to combat as well as support units. Used effectively against logistics depots, rear area support units, and ports of embarkation, biological weapons can be extremely effective.[20] According to the commander of the U.S. Army Chemical and Biological Defense Agency (CBDA), "The biological threat has been recently singled out as the one major threat that still poses the ability for catastrophic effects on a theater-deployed force."[21]

In practice, however, the characteristics of these biological weapons make them difficult to use on the battlefield. They provide wide-area coverage, rather than precision targeting; their effects are harder to control and predict than those of nuclear weapons; and they generally act more slowly than chemical weapons. Technical problems, such as controlling distribution and keeping certain agents alive during dissemination, might result in less damage than expected from biological attacks by small states. Nonetheless, U.S. forces need to be prepared to cope with biological warfare threats on the battlefield, given the proliferation of this potentially lethal and relatively inexpensive capability to regional states who may see BW as a "poor man's atom bomb" to be used to offset U.S. military advantages.[22]

The key to BW protection is for troops to use respirator masks to avoid breathing airborne agents. Most important biological agents are respirable and not "dermally active" (i.e., they tend not to enter through the skin). Accordingly, special protective garments for the entire body are less essential than in the case of chemical attacks.[23]

To be effective, early detection of a BW attack is required so troops can don masks and other protective gear as appropriate. Unfortunately, it is difficult to detect BW clouds which move rapidly and are hard to differentiate from organic material in the air. Thus, U.S. forces may not know they are being subjected to a BW attack until after casualties begin to occur. Nonetheless, taking protective steps at that stage may still be useful for troops not yet exposed. Complicating the situation is the fact that certain BW agents can take days or even weeks to achieve full effect on exposed personnel. Decontamination and medical treatment procedures can mitigate the effects of BW attacks, but neither of these measures is as effective as in the case of CW attacks.

Another BW countermeasure is vaccination of troops. Unlike masks and other protective gear which provide generic protection, immunization presupposes a knowledge of the precise BW threat, availability of a vaccine, and enough time to allow antibodies to be developed (from as low as four to as long as fifteen weeks). Some vaccinations need to applied many times.

Reliance on immunization raises a host of technical, strategic, political, legal, and economic questions[24]:

- What BW threats should be countered (there are 20 serious airborne agents but only anthrax inoculations are authorized)?

- When should troops be given their immunization (in peacetime, early in a conflict, before embarking)?
- Who should receive vaccinations (all forces or some forces and should this be mandatory)?
- Can we have sufficient quantities to implement a meaningful immunization program (a costly effort which is complicated by the fact that some vaccines cannot be stored for long periods)?

To improve protection against BW attacks, an integrated program should be pursued to develop improved BW detectors, acquire specialized BW masks, provide advance inoculations to specially-trained forces, pursue research on new and approved BW vaccines, devise new decontamination and treatment techniques, and ensure that U.S. forces have the doctrine and training to operate in a BW environment.

Chemical Weapons

Chemical weapons are toxic substances that can injure, incapacitate, or kill personnel. In a military setting, they are substantially less lethal than nuclear or biological weapons and may be no more effective than conventional weapons. Moreover, the effects of chemical attacks are often unpredictable and uncontrollable, since success is highly dependent on such factors as weather and terrain.

Still, these low cost and widely available weapons can have serious consequences when used against U.S. forces.[25] Although they do not destroy physical targets, chemical weapons can kill, incapacitate, or terrorize personnel and interfere with military operation by contaminating key areas or equipment. If used properly, chemical weapons can cause disruption and dispersion of troops, weaken forward and rear positions, and potentially make air bases and ports unusable for period of time.

Current CW countermeasures are available in the form of protective suits or MOPP (Mission Oriented Protective Postures), which include gas masks and full-body protective gear to avoid absorption through the skin of chemical substances. But not all units are MOPP-equipped and -trained. Furthermore, existing CW protective suits tend to be hot and bulky, decrease mobility and flexibility, and generally degrade a soldier's ability to perform assigned tasks.[26]

Given the prospect of CW attacks, U.S. forces face the dilemma of whether to move into a MOPP posture and degrade normal battlefield effectiveness or risk being exposed to chemical rounds if tactical warning of incoming attacks is insufficient. By simply threatening to use chemical weapons, an enemy can place U.S. forces in a disadvantageous position.

What is needed is the development of low-cost, lightweight, protective gear for dealing with CW attacks, consistent with the flexibility and mobility of modern U.S. forces. Decontamination techniques and procedures also need to be improved to minimize casualties and mitigate the operational effects of chemical attacks. Sheltered facilities for equipment and personnel can help forces "ride out" chemical attacks. Unlike nuclear and biological strikes, chemical weapons attacks can entail a relatively continuous barrage of large amounts of substances aimed at multiple targets. Protection of personnel and restoration of combat effectiveness in such an environment requires careful preparation and substantial logistics support.

Whether facing chemical, biological, or nuclear attacks, the efficacy of any passive defense measure requires accurate and timely intelligence on the size and type of particular threats, how these weapons will be delivered, where the enemy will strike, and when attacks will occur. Perfect intelligence on these matters can never be achieved. But without some reliable prior information on the nature, scope, and timing of potential NBC attacks, U.S. forces will either be caught off guard without passive defenses in place or have to implement countermeasures in advance—a costly step that can degrade conventional operations and demoralize personnel.

Doctrine and Training

U.S. military forces are guided by doctrinal concepts and principles which provide joint forces "a common perspective from which to plan and operate, and fundamentally shapes the way we prepare for conflicts and other operations."[27] When facing an NBC-armed enemy, U.S. forces must be prepared to revise their strategic objectives, shift their tactics, and employ different concepts of operation. The purpose of these adjustments is to limit damage to forces if NBC weapons were used against them, while continuing to effectively prosecute a regional conflict or accomplish a military operation other than war (MOOTW).

A comprehensive doctrine to guide U.S. forces facing NBC armed opponents should cover such issues as deterrence policy, offensive and defensive countermeasures, operational principles, logistics and medical support, and command, control, and communications. The document "Joint Doctrine for Nuclear, Biological, and Chemical (NBC) Defense," issued in 1994 by the JCS, goes a long way in providing this guidance.[28]

Two doctrinal aspects of dealing with NBC threats might warrant greater attention in U.S. military planning: dispersal of forces and fighting from a distance.

Force Dispersal

In connection with major regional conflicts (MRCs), U. S. ground, air, and sea-based forces tend to follow the basic principle of concentration of capabilities and massing of firepower. This allows us to dictate the time and place of a campaign, penetrate enemy defenses, and keep fatalities low. Similarly, we tend to favor large, dense, and centralized ports and air bases, given the volume of logistics throughput required and the need for sophisticated support to theater-based aircraft. In addition, a few concentrated areas can be more easily secured and defended than many dispersed areas. In our peacetime postures, when forward-deployed on foreign bases or conducting presence operations offshore with naval forces, we also favor sizable configurations. Only for certain limited operations—such as surgical strikes or noncombatant operations (NECs)—do we employ smaller, less concentrated forces.

Unfortunately, massed forces and dense concentrations of military capabilities provide lucrative targets for NBC weapons of any type. Dispersal, on the other hand, can help forces minimize damage, restore their capabilities, and regroup to continue the campaign.[29]

But reorientation of the present approach to regional warfare has its risks and costs. Dispersed forces require extremely mobile systems, more demanding C^3I, and more complex and potentially more expensive logistics. Premature movements from a massed to dispersed posture in anticipation of NBC attacks can also lead to inefficiencies in conducting conventional conflict. Even so, greater attention should be paid to developing dispersal options for joint forces preparing to fight in an NBC environment, even though this may run counter to prevailing doctrine.[30]

Fighting from a Distance

In the post-Cold War era, U.S. military forces have prepared for regional wars and littoral operations, rather than global conflicts. A primary feature of these contingencies is to insert U.S. forces on the ground, base tactical aircraft in theater, and deploy naval forces close to shore. To be sure, we have conducted limited stand-off attacks from a distance, such as TLAM strikes against Iraq, and long-range strategic bombers were used in Desert Storm. But the thrust of U.S. military policy is to remain forward-engaged in peacetime and to deploy additional forces promptly to a conflict area in the event of a crisis that threatens U.S. interests.

When facing an NBC-armed regional opponent, however, proximity could bring U.S. forces within reach of chemical, biological, or nuclear delivery systems. Although deterrence of NBC use could be enhanced by the visible presence of U.S. forces, their greater vulnerability could stimulate an enemy to employ NBC weapons in the hope of disrupting our campaign and weakening our will. U.S. forces deployed in dense formations close to an enemy could create particularly attractive targets.

As in the case of dispersion, it would be advisable to develop new technologies and concepts that could offer options for conducting more effective stand-off operations. These initiatives could include improved accuracy of air- and sea-launched missiles, enhanced techniques for rapid insertion and removal of special forces, and more capable intelligence and battle damage assessments.

Training to Fight

Training for NBC operations goes hand in hand with doctrine. To the degree practicable, all U.S. forces should be trained to view the NBC threat "as an expected condition of conflict and prepare themselves to fight and win under those conditions."[31] The principles contained in the approved JCS publication on NBC doctrine should guide the training programs of all four services.

Before handing-off forces to the regional CINCs, CINCLANTFLT should train deploying Joint Task Forces to deal with NBC threats and develop Adaptive Joint Force Packages capable of fighting in an NBC environment. Joint training should be continued under the auspices of the regional CINCs who are being given greater responsibilities in planning for NBC deterrence and warfighting.[32] The functional CINCs can also play a role in preparing U.S. forces to deal with regional NBC threats.[33]

Another approach is to form specialized units capable of responding to NBC contingencies. This may not prepare U.S. forces for major conflicts where NBC weapons are employed, but can provide rapid reactions to deal with small incidents on a global basis. Such specialized units could also reinforce larger U.S. forces facing

NBC adversaries and apply their expertise to assist regular units in adopting appropriate countermeasures. A creative step in this direction is the decision taken by the U.S. Marine Corps to form a "Bio/Chem Defense Response Unit." This unit of approximately 300 personnel would have the equipment, skills, and organization necessary to deal with terrorist or other localized chemical or biological attacks against command and headquarters facilities at home or abroad.[34]

Although doctrinal publications, improved training, and specialized units represent significant steps towards providing U.S. forces with anti-NBC capabilities, what is required is the introduction of NBC issues into the Defense Planning Guidance (DPG), the Joint Strategic Capabilities Plan (JSCP), and the war plans used by the regional CINCs. Only if NBC requirements appear prominently in these documents can they become meaningful competitors for defense resources and be accepted by the military establishment as necessary for meeting future U.S. security challenges.

The Way Ahead

In his Fiscal Year '95 Posture Statement, the Secretary of Defense said that the Department of Defense "is determined to fulfill its responsibilities in the government-wide effort to deal with the danger posed by the proliferation of weapons of mass destruction, . . . specifically the development of military capabilities to confront a regional opponent armed with these weapons."[35] A short while later, the so-called "Deutch Report" was submitted to Congress, summarizing the counterproliferation technology programs of the DOD and other Executive Branch Agencies.[36] More recently, other initiatives demonstrate that the U.S. defense establishment is taking steps to deter NBC threats and prepare to fight in an NBC environment if necessary. Examples of these initiatives include the issuance of Joint Pub. 3-11 on doctrine for NBC defense, the JCS-coordinated study on missions and functions for organizing DOD counterproliferation efforts, and the formation of a specific group to develop joint counterproliferation systems, requirements, and procurement recommendations.[37]

However, counterproliferation remains a relatively low priority item in the overall DOD budget and is not receiving priority attention in defense planning. This is to be expected in a period of shrinking military resources, where relatively low probability events, such as regional conflicts actually involving NBC use, take back seats to more traditional and continuing defense requirements.[38]

To further improve the ability of U.S. forces to deal with regional NBC threats requires a four-part strategy consisting of the following elements:

1. *Legitimizing NBC deterrence and warfighting as a priority military mission.* Top DOD officials should publicize the significance of the NBC mission and issue formal directives to this effect. Practical signs that priority is being placed on this area should be reflected in greater defense spending on counterproliferation force acquisition and training. Operational commanders at the CINC and Joint Task Force levels need to make NBC warfare prominent in their plans and readiness activities. The Military Service Chiefs and Service Secretaries need to play a particularly active role in the legitimization process, given their Title 10 responsibilities for training and equipping U.S. military forces.

2. *Procuring NBC-relevant weapons systems and equipment.* While pieces of a comprehensive program are in place or underway, what is lacking is a balanced and synergistic procurement strategy covering the multi-tiered steps needed to prepare U.S. forces for NBC deterrence and warfighting. Areas for priority attention include reconnaissance-strike systems to target and destroy deployed NBC weapons, acceleration of area-wide TMD programs, development of BW sensors and vaccination policies, and acquisition of lightweight chemical warfare protection suits. To avoid competing with traditional programs, it would be wise to find either multi-

purpose weapons that can perform NBC missions or relatively inexpensive and specialized NBC-unique items.

3. *Enhancing the training of U.S. forces to deal with NBC threats.* Training should be offered at all levels to all forces, active and reserve. NBC threats, countermeasures, and doctrinal principles should be included in courses at the service and joint schools, embedded in field training at the various training commands, and highlighted in major exercises at home and in overseas areas wherever U.S. forces are stationed. Combined training and exercise evolutions should be held with like-minded friends and allies to prepare for potential coalition operations against common NBC opponents. Advanced training could be given to certain individuals or units, with the prospect of designating NBC a "specialized warfare area" within each service and in the joint community.

4. *Institutionalizing responsibilities for NBC planning and operations.* The recently-completed JCS missions and functions study gives the regional CINCs greater responsibility in developing requirements for NBC missions. This makes sense, since NBC threats need to be dealt with through regional strategies. It is also consistent with the power of the regional CINCs under the Goldwater-Nichols Act.[39] To complement the increased CINC role in NBC planning, it might be advisable to establish the position of Special Assistant to the Chairman of the JCS for NBC matters, with the goal of coordinating service policies and programs. Finally, DOD should implement the recommendation by the CORM that the Under Secretary of Defense for Policy form a coordinating committee to combat proliferation, with the goal of focussing and integrating DoD-wide efforts.[40] Given the importance of buttressing policy with programs, consideration should be given to making the Under Secretary of Defense for Acquisition the co-chairman of this committee.

If these steps are pursued with vigor over a sustained period of time, U.S. military forces will be able to meet the emerging challenge of regional NBC threats. As we move down this path, our friends and allies would be reassured and our adversaries put on notice that we will not be intimidated by attempts to offset our military power through acquisition of NBC weapons. Indeed, if developing a credible U.S. military capability to deal with NBC threats helps dissuade prospective proliferators from seeking these weapons, our investment would be more than justified.

Notes

1. For a discussion of NBC proliferation dynamics and threat projections see *Proliferation of Weapons of Mass Destruction: Assessing the Risks*, Report by the Office of Technology Assessment (OTA), Washington, D.C., August 1993.

2. For purposes of this paper, we assume that NBC-armed regional states will not be able to pose a direct threat to CONUS.

3. In the Gulf War, we suspected that Iraq had programs in various stages of maturity, but we did not believe that U.S. forces would face an operational NBC threat. Would we have intervened if Iraq had been known to have operational nuclear as well as chemical and biological weapons deployed on SCUD mobile missiles?

4. To bound the scope of this paper, the focus will be limited to NBC threats against U.S. forces deployed or arriving overseas and the bases and other support facilities used by U.S. forces. How the U. S. deals with regional NBC threats directed against the forces, bases, or cities of allies or coalition partners who may be fighting with us or hosting U.S. forces raises a different set of issues.

5. Many regional states acquire NBC capabilities for use as psychological or political weapons, hoping that U.S. forces might "turn tail" or that U.S. political leaders will disengage due to domestic concerns over the prospect of massive casualties caused by "horrible" means, notably nuclear or biological weapons.

6. This discussion is drawn from a more detailed treatment of deterrence found in "Regional Deterrence Strategies for New Proliferation Threats," by Jerome H. Kahan, a paper prepared for a National Defense University (NDU) Working Group on June 19, 1995.

7. The U.S. no longer has biological warfare capabilities and has agreed to dismantle its chemical warfare capabilities.

8. No one has forgotten that, whatever the justification, the U.S. remains the only nation to have used nuclear weapons "in anger."

9. President Clinton put the world on notice that "we will retain strategic nuclear forces sufficient to deter any hostile foreign leadership" with nuclear weapons "from acting against our vital interests" and "will continue to maintain nuclear forces of sufficient size and capability to hold at risk a broad range of assets valued by such political and military leaders." *A National Security Strategy of Engagement and Enlargement*, July 1994. In a more focused but still ambiguous statement, the President threatened to respond "with all means necessary" against North Korea if that country uses nuclear weapons. "U.S. Warns North Korea on Nuclear Weapons," *The Washington Post*, July 11, 1993, p. A-19.

10. One potential constraint on the exercising of this option is the so-called "negative security assurance" statement issued by the U.S in 1978. In essence, this affirms that the U.S. will not initiate nuclear use against any state that does not have nuclear weapons if that state is a member in good standing of the NPT, unless the nation in question commits aggression against the U.S., its forces, or its allies in association with a nuclear-armed state. While constraining U.S. nuclear first use, this formulation is open to interpretation and provides considerable latitude in justifying such an act.

11. Regional states are more likely to use or threaten to use nuclear arms as weapons of last resort to protect their regimes from being overthrown. One option would be to launch a nuclear "demonstration shot" in the hope of intimidating our forces or frightening our leaders.

12. This formulation was developed by players in the NBC Cell during the Global '95 Wargame at Newport, Rhode Island, in July 1995.

13. For an overview of the relative effectiveness of NBC weapons see, OTA Report, pp. 46-58.

14. Although intelligence and targeting capabilities have improved, the difficulties faced by the U.S. in locating and destroying Iraqi mobile SCUD missiles during the Gulf War underscore this point.

15. For an explanation of "balance" in designing defenses against different modes of NBC attack, see Alexander Flax, "Implementations of Defenses Against Tactical Ballistic Missiles," *Arms Control Today*, May 1994, pp. 6-10.

16. For a discussion of the potential role of U.S. active defense systems in regional nuclear crises see *The Impact of Nuclear Proliferation*, Analyses (CRM-94-69), by Thomas J. Hirschfeld, et al, July 1995, pp. 59-62.

17. See "Post-Cold War deterrence and Missile Defense" by Keith Payne in *ORBIS*, Spring 1995, pp. 201-223, and "Inside Missile Defense," September 27, 1995, for summaries of current U.S. TMD plans and programs.

18. See statements by the Director of Central Intelligence on the emerging third world ballistic missile threats (March 17, 1994 and February 24, 1993) as cited in *U.S. Ballistic Missile Defense Program*, DoD/BMDO, October 1994.

19. The U.S. Army defines passive defense as "measures to reduce the vulnerability of one's forces to . . . [NBC attacks] or minimize the effect of a strike on that force." *Weapons of Mass Destruction: Title 10 implications for the Military*, CSI, U.S. Army War College, August 1994.

20. One study observes that "biological weapons are so potent that, under conditions favorable to the attacker, they can kill as many people as comparably sized-nuclear weapons." OTA Report, p. 8.

21. Brig. Gen. George Friel, Commanding General, U.S. Army CBCA, quoted in John G. Roos, "Chem-Bio Defense Agency Will Tackle 'Last Major Threat to a Deployed Force,'" *Armed Forces Journal International*, December 1992, p.10.

22. Statement by Iranian leader Rafsanjani in 1988, cited by W. Seth Carus in "Proliferation in the Middle East: A Regional Perspective," paper prepared for an NDU Workshop, May 19, 1995, p. 9.

23. *Defense Against Toxic Weapons*, Col. David R. Franz, Veterinary Corps, U.S. Army, 1994.

24. See DOD Directive 6205.3, Immunization Program for Biological Warfare Defense, November 29, 1993.

25. See "Chemwar in the Third World" by Colleen A. Nash, *Air Force Magazine*, Vol. 73, Number 1, January 1990.

26. See OTA Report, p. 36.

27. *Doctrine for Joint Operations*, Joint Pub. 3-0, Message from the Chairman, JCS, 9 September 1993.

28. Joint Pub. 3-11, 15 April 1994.

29. Positioning U.S. Forces in dispersed formations to deal with NBC attacks is not new. In his FY '56 Annual Budget Message to Congress, President Eisenhower announced that the U.S. Army was to be organized into smaller, more mobile units "capable of meeting the conditions of the atomic battlefield." These so-called Pentomic Divisions deployed in Europe

were replaced by more traditional formations in the 1960's.

30. Despite the logic of dispersal, a CNA study observed that in Desert Storm, U.S. and allied forces, aware that Iraq had chemical weapons and an aggressive employment doctrine, still concentrated air power at selected bases. *The Impact of Nuclear Proliferation*, p. 82.

31. *Weapons of Mass Destruction*, p. viii.

32. See discussion of the role of the regional CINCs in Kahan, "Regional Strategies".

33. For example, STRATCOM is assisting regional CINCs in developing targeting lists against NBC capabilities located in selected third-world adversary states. *Inside the Pentagon*, Vol. 10, No. 50, December 15, 1995

34. This concept is still being refined but is scheduled to go into operation by April 1996. It was put forth in the Commandants' Planning Guidance of July 1996 and is described in various draft activation plans being produced at MCCDC.

35. *Annual Report to the President and Congress*, Secretary of Defense, Les Aspen, January 1994, p. 35.

36. *Report on Nonproliferation and Counterproliferation Activities and Programs*, Office of the Deputy Secretary of Defense, May 1994.

37. There is currently a dedicated Joint War Force Capabilities Assessment (JWCA) for counterproliferation coordinated by the Joint Staff. This group's recommendations are considered by the Joint Requirements Oversight Council (JROC) and, if approved by the Chairman of the JCS, becomes input to the Secretary of Defense's Defense Planning Guidance (DPG) which in turn provides strategy and force requirements guidance to the military services.

38. While existing counterproliferation technology and acquisition programs are being pursued, it is reported that "development of a full-fledged counterproliferation acquisition plan has been slowed by the absence of military requirements and the reluctance of service leaders to make room in their budgets for new priorities identified by Pentagon policy-makers." *Defense News*, November 6-12, 1995, p. 20.

39. See Kahan "Regional Strategies" for a discussion of the role of the regional CINCS and the elements of a regional NBC deterrence strategy.

40. *Directions for Defense: Report of the Commission on Roles and Missions of the Armed Forces*, 24 May 1995.

◆ Deterring the Use of Weapons of Mass Destruction:

Lessons from History

KEITH B. PAYNE

The identification of "how to deter" the use of weapons of mass destruction, in practice, is a question of how to deter an opposing leadership from extreme provocations under specific circumstances. The size and type of the U.S. threat, and how, when, and to whom it should be communicated will be shaped by the context and the character of the opponent. If an opponent can be subjected to deterrence pressure, to deter WMD the United States will need to understand the type of necessary threat, how to make that threat credible, and delineate for the opponent's vivid understanding that WMD use is the behavior that the opponent must avoid. Because

Keith B. Payne is President, National Institute for Public Policy, Georgetown University.

the incentive to use WMD varies by opponent, and more importantly, because the contextual factors absolutely essential to deterrence "working" vary, U.S. deterrence capabilities and policies will have to be extremely flexible. They will have to be tailored to suit the occasion and specific opponent. To the extent that U.S. flexibility is constrained by the wholesale elimination of relevant U.S. military capabilities, or by placing selected U.S. capabilities "in the background," the U.S. capacity for deterrence may be reduced. In short, the first lessons of history for deterrence in the post-Cold War period are: 1) U.S. intelligence capabilities will be critical because they will provide the basis for tailoring the U.S. deterrent policy to the specific situation; and 2) U.S. deterrence policies will require significant flexibility in application, including with regard to the U.S. threat and how it may be communicated.

U.S. improvising during the Gulf War to deter Iraqi chemical warfare (CW) use suggests the deterrence value of flexibility in policy, the importance of delineating explicitly the behavior that the opponent must avoid, and tailoring communications and threat to the context and the opponent. The relatively explicit U.S. (and Israeli) nuclear threats in this case offer some tentative indication that nuclear threats may substitute for the threats of retaliation-in-kind that appear to have deterred some CW use in the past. Ultimately, however, whether conventional threats can be adequate for deterrence of WMD, or whether nuclear, chemical, or biological warfare threats will be necessary, will be determined by U.S. intelligence, skill in implementing policy, the character of the opponent, and the context.

The difficulties involved in identifying deterrence strategies in which confidence can be placed strongly recommends policies of deterrence by denial as opposed to punitive deterrence. In the absence of clear guidance to the contrary, denial deterrence will provide both the possibility for deterrence and a hedge against its failure.

Finally, one of the self-declared reasons for the acquisition of WMD by developing states is the desire to deter the United States from regional intervention. To provide the basis for the credibility of the U.S. deterrent threat in such cases, the U.S. leadership must not be perceived as vulnerable to the opponent's coercion. This suggests strongly the importance for U.S. policies of deterrence of a U.S. capability to counter an opponent's WMD —again, a reason for moving toward deterrence by denial unless strong evidence suggests otherwise.

Deterring the Use of Weapons of Mass Destruction: Lessons from History[1]

The Department of Defense Dictionary defines deterrence as, "The prevention from action by fear of the consequences. Deterrence is a state of mind brought about by the existence of a credible threat of unacceptable counter action." While this definition does not acknowledge requirements beyond "a credible threat of unacceptable counter action,"[23] to bring about deterrence, it does properly highlight the important fact that deterrence is a psychological function, a "state of mind"—not the automatic result of any combination of forces and threats, however fearsome they may seem.

As a policy, deterrence is a conscious attempt to influence an opponent's calculations of anticipated costs and gains in a manner that leads it away from unwanted decisions and actions.

Typically, deterrence threats are intended to shape an opposing leadership's decisionmaking in a preferred direction by leading that leadership to calculate that the costs of aggression will outweigh anticipated gains. Those "costs" may be punitive. That is, they may involve threats to an opponent's values as opposed to threats that would, if executed, serve a military purpose. In contrast, threats may be issued in terms of denying an opponent its military goals. The former approach typically is referred to a deterrence by punishment; the latter is deterrence by denial.

In either case, the opponent decides whether or not it can and will be deterred. The success of a deterrence policy ultimately is determined by the opponent's calculations and decisionmaking.

During the Cold War the United States established a deterrence relationship with the Soviet Union based on a combination of punitive and denial threats. The ultimate declared U.S. punitive threat was the "assured destruction" of the Soviet Union. The officially-declared definition of this assured destruction threat evolved over time—from large-scale urban and industrial destruction to the reportedly more counter-economic and -political targeting concepts of the 1970s and 1980s.[4]

With the collapse of the Soviet Union and the proliferation of missiles and weapons of mass destruction (WMD) to a growing list of regional powers, previous U.S. approaches to deterrence that suited the Cold War need to be reviewed for their relevance to the potential WMD threats that the United States could face in the future.[5] An analysis of numerous historical case studies provides some "lessons" concerning the question of "how to deter" in a period no longer dominated by ideologically-defined bipolar political alliances. Most of the "lessons of history" concern deterrence in general. There is little historical basis for disaggregating nuclear, chemical, and biological threats and confidently drawing specific conclusions about the specific requirements to deter the use of each separate from the other or even from the deterrence of conflict in general. However, because deterrence is a process of influencing the decisionmaking of an opposing leadership, it is possible to identify some of the general lessons of history, and extrapolate their meaning for the deterrence of leaders who are armed with WMD. And, in some cases, specific lessons may be gleaned from the historical record.

An initial point suggested by historical studies is that some potential challengers simply will not respond predictably to U.S. policies of deterrence. The most obvious case in which deterrence cannot function by design is one in which the opposing leadership is unable to formulate decisions rationally.

"Rationality," as used in deterrence considerations, is not necessarily synonymous with Western interpretations of "reasonable" or "sensible." Opponents can be rational on their own terms, logically linking behavior with goals, but doing so in the context of very different value hierarchies. Such opponents may wrongly be labeled irrational because Western leaders have difficulty understanding their goals and their decisions in support of those goals; consequently their behavior is unpredictable, if not irrational.

Nevertheless, deterrence concepts and policies require rational opponents or there exists no basis for anticipating behavior—an irrational opponent could respond in a completely unpredictable manner to a deterrent threat. Whether the result of an individual leader's psychosis, or the result of other possible impediments to rational decision-making, an opposing leadership that effectively is irrational cannot be deterred by design because its reaction to deterrence threats will be unpredictable, even unfathomable.

U.S. leaders facing an effectively irrational opponent might be fortunate in that the opponent's decision-making and behavior could, by chance as opposed to design, be influenced as hoped by U.S. threats. However, identifying in advance a particular deterrence policy that will "work" by chance against an irrational opponent will not be possible. In such cases, luck will be the essential ingredient in a successful deterrence policy.

It should be noted that the incidence of leaders suffering from psychopathology historically does not appear to be high. Leaders such as Stalin, Hitler, Ludwig II of Bavaria, and England's Henry VI and George III appear to have been so afflicted. Nevertheless, more common than irrationality is the unexpected behavior of rational leaders, whose decisionmaking is impaired by faulty information, poor judgment, and several well-understood psychological mechanisms that can impede a rational leader's capacity to make decisions in a fully informed and purely rational manner.

We know that in crisis situations, decisions tend to be based on fairly simplified cognitive structures, which tend to reduce the range of options perceived by the leaders involved.[6] Also, there is no doubt that objective rationality in decisionmaking can be impaired by various psychological defense mechanisms.[7] One example of the type of psychological factors that appears to have led rational leaders to such miscalculation is the *denial* mechanism. Denial can affect a person who is compelled to choose among a panoply of difficult options. A choice is made, and the decisionmaker subsequently simply denies the possible negative consequences associated with the chosen course and ignores information suggesting negative consequences associated with that choice.

Denial is a basic human psychological reaction to danger and involves "various degrees of nonperception, nonrecognition, nonunderstanding, or nonacceptance of certain realities...."[8] Detailed historical case studies suggest that psychological defense mechanisms such as denial have indeed played in miscalculations that resulted in the outbreak of crises and wars during both the nuclear and pre-nuclear age.[9]

Another case in which deterrence cannot function predictably is when an opposing leadership (of a state or non-state organization) places supreme importance on a particular goal, and believes a specific course of action to be essential to the attainment of that goal. In this case we are dealing with the factor of determination and will. In this situation, again, no deterrence policy will successfully discourage that leadership from the action it perceives as indispensable to its overriding goal. When leaders are wholly committed to achieving a goal "at any cost," then deterrence cannot operate as intended because no threats are likely to be sufficient to deter the actions deemed essential to that goal. In such cases, opposing leaders may appear "irrational" because even credible threats will not determine their decisions and actions.[10] The situation described here, which does appear historically with some regularity, is not necessarily one of irrationality. Rather, a leadership is so committed to its goal that it can, quite rationally, decide to accept any level of risk in pursuit of the goal. Historically, statements reflecting such a level of determination have been expressed relatively frequently, including in the United States: as American revolutionary Josiah Quincy (1744-1775) proclaimed in *Observations on the Boston Port Bill* (the first of the British "Intolerable Acts"): "Blandishments will not fascinate us, nor will threats of a 'halter' intimidate, for, under God, we are determined that wheresoever, whensoever, or howsoever we shall be called to make our exit, we will die free men."[11]

Prior to the Gulf War, Saddam Hussein expressed statements that also indicated a willingness to accept high risks in pursuit of particular goals:

> If you use pressure, we will deploy pressure and force. We know that you can harm us, although we do not threaten you. But we too can harm you. . . .You can come to Iraq with aircraft and missiles, but do not push us to the point where we cease to care. And when we feel that you want to injure our pride and take away the Iraqis' chance of a high standard of living, then we will cease to care, and death will be the choice for us. Then we would not care if you fired 100 missiles for each missile we fired. Because without pride life would have no value.[12]

The types of goals that have occupied such priority positions have included leadership prestige, political independence, regime survival, ideological commitment, and religious devotion, *inter alia*. Historically, it is clear that deterrence does fail, when it otherwise could be expected to function, when the leadership attempting to deter or the leaders who are the target of the deterrent threat fail to understand their opponent's determination and willingness to accept high, even seemingly suicidal risks.[13]

Consequently, the initial "lesson of history" that applies to deterrence in general (and the deterrence of WMD as a subset) is that the opponent must be vulnerable to U.S. deterrence pressure. That is, the opponent's decisionmaking must be rational, predictable, and U.S. threats must, in each particular case, be decisive in the opponent's cost-benefit calculations. These conditions should not be assumed because challengers may easily make decisions based on mindsets that are not reasonable or sensible according to U.S. standards—and thus surprising to Washington.

Consequently, the initial step in identifying how to deter is to ascertain whether the opponent in question can be subjected to U.S. deterrence threats, and if so, what should be the character of those threats. Beyond the most trivial level of guidance (i.e., U.S. threats should address what the opponent values, and be credible), answers to these questions can not be generalized. Rather, they will be shaped by the unique circumstances of the opponent, the context, and the "stakes" involved.

This initial requirement to identify if the opponent can be subjected to U.S. deterrent pressure, and if so what threats will be effective, presupposes other necessary conditions for deterrence, e.g., the capability of the U.S. leadership involved to communicate with the appropriate people on the other side. U.S. leaders must have at their disposal effective communication channels to inform the opposing leadership, at least in general terms, of the existence of a deterrent threat, the conditions under which that threat will be withheld/executed (i.e., what is acceptable/unacceptable behavior), and the degrees of commitment involved. This latter information concerning commitment can shape to a significant degree, for example, the level of credibility that an opponent attaches to a deterrent threat and, therefore, the effectiveness of the threat.

Communicating such information can, of course, be through a mixture of actions and declarations. How communications are presented, and by whom, can shape the opponent's response. For example, in some political cultures, greater significance would likely be placed on a message delivered by a close relative of the U.S. President, than if it were delivered by a local U.S. official or even a senior official from Washington. And, as Alexander George has noted, in some cultures leaders respond "very negatively indeed" to being threatened directly.[14] Consequently, part of the initial step in understanding how to deter, is to understand how to communicate with the particular leadership in question, with an appreciation of how politics and culture will shape its perceptions.

Communication need not be precise—in some cases both parties may seek a level of ambiguity in these areas. For example, the leadership attempting to deter may avoid specifying the precise provocation that would lead to execution of the deterrent threat in the hope that the threat will be effective over a wider range of provocations than it would, in fact, wish to specify. This tactic of intended ambiguity has been used by the United States. For example, U.S. declarations regarding strategic "launch under attack" were ambiguous by design. Ambiguity may be useful; it also may have the unintended effect of encouraging a risk-tolerant opponent to interpret ambiguity as signifying an exploitable softness in commitment.

While communication of such information may be incomplete and general, it must at least establish that the leaderships are in a deterrence relationship and a level of credibility behind the deterrent in the eyes of the opponent. Effective communication by design, of course, requires that the leaders involved know with whom and how to communicate.

In short, for deterrence to "work" by design requires rationality, effective communication between the leaderships involved, an opponent who is deterrable and predictable, and a threat that is sufficiently lethal and credible to be decisive in the opponent's cost-benefit calculations. Deterrence can take place in the absence of these conditions. That is, a leadership may be deterred by its own internally-generated estimate of the risks involved in a given situation, independent of its opponent's efforts to deter. Such occasions, however, represent deterrence by happenstance, not by design, and cannot serve as the basis for a policy of deterrence.

These historically derived "lessons" have several significant implications for post-Cold War deterrence in general, and for deterrence of WMD. For example, whether attempting to establish the basis for deterring conflict in general or WMD specifically, the United States must ascertain:

(1) whether the opponent is capable of rational decision-making;

(2) whether there is sufficient softness in the opponent's determination for a U.S. threat to pose an effective deterrent;

(3) what are the characteristics of a potentially effective threat, if such a threat is possible, and how may it be made credible to the opponent;

(4) how and to whom can such an effective threat be communicated.

Establishing a U.S. deterrence policy that meets these requirements will necessitate the tailoring of that policy to the given opponent and context based on substantial intelligence about the opponent in question.[15] It simply is not possible to suggest as a general principle that a specific formula exists for deterring rogue states from conflict, or WMD use—whether that formula involves conventional and/or nuclear threats—however severe U.S. leaders might consider their threat to be. The differences in leaderships, their decision-making processes, risk-tolerances, threat perceptions, goals, values and determination, and simply the potential for idiosyncratic behavior, must limit the value of any general formula for deterrence of conflict or WMD use.

Whether the U.S. deterrent functions as hoped will be determined by many factors, including how that U.S. threat is understood and assessed by the opponent, the character of its decisionmaking process, its determination, and its propensity for risk-taking over the issues in question. Of these various factors that shape the effectiveness of a deterrent threat, the United States may have the capacity through its declarations and actions to influence the opponent's estimation of the threat and the conditions leading to its execution or avoidance. The United States may have little or no influence over other important factors.

The degree to which the effectiveness of a deterrent threat is "in the hands" of the opponent is suggested by a conclusion from one of the foremost historical analysis of threats: "If one does not threaten the right target, for the right reasons, it may not matter how well one does it."[16]   Consequently, for those cases in which an opponent can in fact be deterred, to design an effective deterrent against conflict in general or a more specific act such as WMD use, the U.S. leadership must have a substantial intelligence information base concerning the specific country, leadership, and context involved. With adequate intelligence, the United States may improve the prospects for establishing an effective deterrent to conflict in general and WMD use in particular. It must seek to identify what threat is suitable for the leadership and context in question, and how to communicate that threat and its credibility. U.S. leaders must also be able to inform the opponent of the behavior that must be avoided if it wishes to avoid the U.S. deterrent threat.   Ultimately, it is U.S. leaders who will have to establish whether the behavior that must be avoided by the opponent is conflict in general, the use of WMD, or a particular variety of WMD. The question of deterring WMD will not be one of finding a generic threat suitable for deterring a generic opponent's nuclear use, CW use or BW use, with separate formulas for deterrence based on the type of WMD threat.

Rather, the issue is one of identifying the type of deterrent necessary for different adversaries and contexts, i.e., designing a deterrent policy suited to the particular opponent and context. A deterrence policy intended to prevent extreme provocations must communicate to the opponent that WMD use is at least part of the extreme behavior that must be avoided. If the opponent is vulnerable to U.S. deterrence pressure, the challenge is to understand how to communicate suitable U.S. threats and thresholds credibly to that opponent. If done, U.S. leaders will be in the position to deter the extreme provocations they specify as unacceptable, whether that provocation is conflict in general or a particular type of WMD use.

The point here is that there is no "natural" distinction among WMD that can be assumed across a variety of opponents that permits the identification of different generic threats or conditions that will deter nuclear, chemical, or biological use. Disaggregation of the threat to be deterred (i.e., attempting to define generic formula for deterring conventional threats as opposed to WMD threats, or nuclear threats, as opposed to BW or CW) can follow from identifying how to deter specific opponents from extreme provocations, and then successfully defining for that opponent that the extreme provocation that it must avoid includes WMD use or a specific type of WMD use.

In short, it is the unique opponent armed with WMD that must be deterred under specific circumstances, not a particular type of WMD. Once it is understood if and how a policy of deterring extreme provocation can be designed for a particular opponent, identifying WMD use as the extreme provocation in question is at the discretion of the U.S. leadership.

The threats required to deter WMD use, or specific types of WMD use across the wide spectrum of prospectively deterrable opponents, are likely to be quite different, with regard to the type of force, use threatened, and the targets selected. This will be the case because of the many differences in the context involved, opponents' goals and intentions, and because different opponents will have different incentives to use nuclear weapons, CW or BW. The U.S. deterrent must speak to these particular opponents and incentives. In some cases, a massive punitive- or denial-oriented conventional threat may be suitable, in others an adequate deterrent may require a proportional nuclear, chemical, or biological threat, in others, a grossly disproportional threat may be needed.

To suggest as a general principle that U.S. conventional threats will be adequate for deterrence because they increasingly can inflict damage equivalent to WMD, or that nuclear threats will be necessary because of their lethality, assumes a similarity among potential opponents and contexts that almost certainly will not exist. It also wrongly assumes that the type of U.S. force use threatened is the only factor shaping deterrent effectiveness. As suggested above, deterrence, properly understood, involves much more than the character of the U.S. threat. Indeed, the severity of the threat is only one of many critical factors. Consequently, an effective U.S. deterrent will be based on the particular type of threat suited to a particular opponent, and it will take into account these additional critical factors. If it fails to do so, the particular character of the U.S. threat may be irrelevant.

This should not be a controversial conclusion. Historical studies concerning deterrence typically reach a similar conclusion:[17] U.S. threats will be perceived differently and inspire different types of responses from different leaderships. Nevertheless, this particular conclusion questions our capability to identify general force requirements in response to the question "how much is enough?" for deterrence of specific cases.

For example, in some cases U.S. nuclear threats may appear credible to an opponent, and be decisive in its decisionmaking. In other cases they may not be judged as credible, or of sufficient concern to be decisive in an opponent's decisionmaking. And, the estimate of credibility by an opponent is not under U.S. control; it may not even be possible for the United States to influence that estimate significantly at the time of a crisis. The perception of U.S. commitment is likely to be shaped by the history of U.S. linkages to a state or region much more than by declarations at the time of a crisis.

It is possible to observe that U.S. deterrence policies suited to particular opponents, as opposed to some generic enemy, will require flexibility on the part of the United States to match particular types of deterrent policies and threats to particular opponents. To the extent that the United States has the widest possible spectrum of capabilities with which to threaten, it increases the probability that it will have at its disposal the necessary type of capability for deterrence. In contrast, to the extent that capabilities are excluded from the U.S. inventory, it reduces U.S. flexibility and places a greater burden on the remaining forces to provide a deterrent for all seasons. This could create some shortcomings in the U.S. deterrence potential.

For example, to deter chemical or biological threats, the United States will increasingly be limited to conventional or nuclear threats in the military sphere. If an opponent armed with BW or CW judges a U.S. conventional threat to be insufficient to be decisive in its decisionmaking, and judges the U.S. nuclear threat as too asymmetrical to be credible, an effective U.S. military deterrent may not be possible in such cases.

Assuming that the United States has the forces necessary in principle to deter WMD, the question will be whether U.S. intelligence on the particular country and leaders in question will be adequate to design an effective deterrence policy. That question will be repeated vis-a-vis the list of opponents that U.S. leaders seek to be capable of deterring. Given the numerous factors that are involved in establishing an effective deterrent relationship, whether one actually can be designed against a particular foe will not easily be surmised in advance.

In the absence of the types of substantive information identified above, there can be no basis for making recommendations regarding the specific deterrence requirements necessary to discourage any particular foe from a specific act. It does not necessarily follow, however, that policies of deterrence should be abandoned when the necessary intelligence base is unavailable or ambiguous.

Rather, U.S. efforts to deter in such cases should be extended in full understanding that deterrence policies may not work, and consequently that U.S. policy should hedge against the possibility of its own failure. That is, when there is an insufficient intelligence base upon which to tailor a specific U.S. deterrent threat, deterrence by denial (i.e., involving U.S. military threats to the opponent's military capabilities and objectives) may provide an adequate basis for deterrence, and could serve as a useful hedge in the event deterrence fails. In this case, the execution of a denial threat could serve a useful purpose—including the physical destruction of the opponent's capabilities, the use of which the deterrence policy was intended to discourage. In short, in the absence of better guidance, deterrence by denial will likely be the prudent approach, providing both the possibility of deterrence and a hedge against its failure.

In such cases, punitive deterrence threats may not only be ill-suited for deterrence purposes, but their actual execution following the failure of deterrence would likely serve little or no useful purpose. (On the other hand, it must be recognized that execution of a *punitive* deterrent threat following deterrence failure—whatever that target set might constitute for the opponent in question—could serve as a means of strengthening the credibility of U.S. deterrent threats for future occasions.)

Despite the difficulties in identifying useful general principles, additional conjecture is possible. For example, some rogue leaders, including Saddam Hussein and Muammar Al-Qadhafi, have stated that they seek WMD and missile delivery systems as a means of deterring U.S. intervention in their region. U.S. threats intended to deter these leaders may be insufficiently credible, if they believe that U.S. military operations can be deterred by their own WMD threats to U.S. forces and/or territory. Consequently, the U.S. capability to counter the deterrent threats posed by some rogue leaders may be key to the credibility, and hence the potential effectiveness, of America's own deterrent threats. The implication of this, again, is that deterrence by denial will be the prudent approach in the absence of intelligence suggesting the contrary.

In addition, some rogue leaders appear to be highly risk-tolerant and the focal point of centralized authority, including, for example, Saddam Hussein. In such cases the most effective U.S. course may be to convey severe deterrence threats at the highest levels. Ambiguity and very constrained expressions may be useless or counterproductive in communicating resolve and a deterrent threat that is decisive in such an opponent's calculations. U.S. protestations to Iraq prior to the invasion of Kuwait in this regard, apparently made by Ambassador April Glaspie, were inadequate to deter invasion.

In contrast, subsequent threats in response to the potential Iraqi use of chemical weapons were relatively explicit, severe, and from senior leaders—and may have served to deter. It should be noted that the establishment of a deterrent threat to Iraqi CW and BW use during the Gulf War was improvised according to the occasion, and not the product of a prestanding generic policy or strategy. The value of such threats for this situation is at least suggested by the Iraqi case. The issue in question, of course, is why Saddam Hussein did not use chemical weapons during the war. Was he deterred, and if so why?

There are several plausible answers to these questions. The answer frequently suggested by Israeli analysts is that the Israeli nuclear threat deterred Iraqi chemical use. In this regard, it should be noted that during a CNN interview on February 2, 1991, U.S. Defense Secretary Cheney was asked about the potential for Israeli nuclear retaliation to Iraqi chemical strikes. Secretary Cheney observed that this would be a decision that, "the Israelis would have to make—but I would think that [Hussein] has to be cautious in terms of how he proceeds in his attacks against Israel." The subsequent day, when asked about Secretary Cheney's statement, Israeli Defense Minister Arens replied, "I think he [Cheney] said that Saddam has reasons to worry—yes, he does have reasons to worry."[18]   This reply, and Secretary Cheney's original statement, in which he did not object to the premise of the question, or express disapproval of the possibility of nuclear use, at least to Israeli analysts, was a key to deterring Iraqi chemical weapons.[19]

The possible direct U.S. role in nuclear deterrence in this case also should be highlighted. On January 9, 1991, Secretary of State Baker expressed a relatively clear and severe deterrent threat to Tariq 'Aziz in Geneva:

> Before we cross to the other side—that is, if the conflict starts, God forbid, and chemical or biological weapons are used against our forces-the American people would demand revenge, and we have the means to implement this.[20]

President Bush also sent a strongly-worded message to Saddam Hussein, in the form of a letter delivered to Tariq 'Aziz by Secretary Baker. This letter stated:

> Let me state, too, that the United States will not tolerate the use of chemical or biological weapons or the destruction of Kuwait's oil fields and installations. . . . The American people would demand the strongest possible response. You and your country will pay a terrible price if you order unconscionable acts of this sort.[21]

Secretary of Defense Cheney linked U.S nuclear threats even more explicitly to Iraqi use of WMD:

> The other point that needs to be made, and it's one I have made previously, is that he [Hussein] needs to be made aware that the President will have available the full spectrum of capabilities. And were Saddam Hussein foolish enough to use weapons of mass destruction, the U.S. response would be absolutely overwhelming and it would be devastating. He has to take that into consideration, it seems to me, before he embarks upon a course of using those kinds of capabilities.[22]

The point here is that deterrence of Iraqi chemical use may have been the result of relatively direct language, severe threats delivered to and from the highest levels, and an absolutely clear delineation of the specific actions U.S. leaders judged to be unacceptable, e.g., Iraqi WMD use. That this accounts for the Iraqi nonuse of CW will remain speculative, of course, unless and until an authoritative account of Iraqi decisionmaking is available.

The above discussion demonstrates that some evidence exists suggesting that nuclear threats, direct communication at the highest levels, and explicit U.S. delineation of its deterrent objective, may have contributed to the deterrence of Iraqi CW attack.

Several additional pre-nuclear cases of chemical use and nonuse provide the basis for additional conjecture on this subject. For example, following the initial experiences with CW in World War I, CW was not used in Europe or by the Japanese against the United States in World War II. These and several additional cases of nonuse typically are attributed, at least in part, to defenses and the deterrent threat of retaliation in kind.[23] In several cases of CW use (e.g., Italian use against Ethiopia in 1935, Japanese use against Chinese forces beginning in 1937, and Egyptian use against Yemen in 1967), the target of CW use essentially was defenseless and incapable of retaliation in kind. While not conclusive by any means, these cases suggest the possibility that the presence of defenses and the capability for retaliation in kind may contribute to the deterrence of CW.

It is unclear whether the U.S. nuclear capability can now effectively replace this apparent deterrent value for a capability to retaliate in kind against a CW threat. The Iraqi case suggests that it may. As emphasized above, however, such a generalization regarding deterrence of CW use can not be drawn with confidence from so few historical experiences. There are similar limitations with regard to generalizations disaggregating nuclear and BW threats.

In summary, the identification of "how to deter" the use of WMD or specific types of WMD, in practice, is a question of how to deter an opposing leadership from extreme provocations under specific circumstances, and effectively defining the extreme provocation the opponent must avoid. Other inhibitions that an opponent may feel restrict its use of WMD—humane and moral concerns or operational complexities and dangers—may discourage use, but are not elements of a U.S. deterrence policy per se.

The size and type of the U.S. threat, and how, when, and to whom it should be communicated will be shaped by the context and the character of the opponent. If an opponent can be subjected to deterrence pressure, the U.S. will need to understand the type of necessary threat, how to make its threat credible, and delineate for the opponent's vivid understanding that WMD use is the behavior that the opponent must avoid. Because the incentive to use these weapons varies, and more importantly, because the contextual factors absolutely essential to deterrence "working" vary, U.S. deterrence capabilities and policies will have to be extremely flexible. To the extent that U.S. flexibility is constrained by the wholesale elimination of relevant capabilities, the U.S. capacity for deterrence may be reduced.

U.S. improvising during the Gulf War to deter Iraqi CW use suggests the deterrence value of flexibility in policy, the importance of delineating explicitly the behavior that the opponent must avoid, and tailoring communications and threat to the context and the opponent. The relatively explicit U.S. (and Israeli) nuclear threats in this case offers some tentative indication that nuclear threats may substitute for the threats of retaliation-in-kind that appear to have deterred some CW use in the past. Ultimately, however, whether conventional threats can be adequate for deterrence of WMD, or whether nuclear, CW, or BW threats will be necessary, will be determined by U.S. intelligence and skill, the character of the opponent, and the context.

The difficulties involved in identifying deterrence strategies in which confidence can be placed strongly recommends policies of denial as opposed to punitive deterrence. In the absence of clear guidance to the contrary, denial deterrence will provide the possibility for deterrence and a hedge against its failure.

Finally, one of the self-declared reasons for the acquisition of WMD by developing states is the desire to deter the United States from regional intervention. To provide the basis for the credibility of the U.S. deterrent threat in such cases, the U.S. leadership must not be perceived as vulnerable to the opponent's coercion. This suggests strongly the importance for deterrence of U.S. capabilities to counter an opponent's WMD capabilities—again, a reason for moving toward deterrence by denial unless strong evidence suggests otherwise.

Notes

1.   This essay draws from numerous studies of deterrence, based on historical case studies, including the author's own such studies, on-going since 1979, and published in, Keith B. Payne and Lawrence Fink, "Deterrence without Defense: Gambling on Perfection," *Strategic Review* (Winter 1989),pp. 25-40; Keith B. Payne, "Munich Fifty Years After," in, U.S. Institute of Peace, *The Meaning of Munich Fifty Years Later* (Washington, D.C.; U.S. Institute of Peace, 1990), pp. 57-69; Keith B. Payne, "Deterrence and U.S. strategic Force Requirements After the Cold War.," *Comparative Strategy,* Vol. 11. No. 3., 1992, pp. 269-282; Keith B. Payne, "Deterrence And The Lessons from History," *Statecraft and Power,* Christopher Harmon,

ed. (Lanham, MD: University Press of America, 1994) and Keith b. Payne, "Post-Cold War Deterrence and Defense," *Orbis* (Spring 1995), 201-223.

2. *Department of Defense Dictionary of Military and Associated Terms,* Joint Pub 1-02 (Washington, D.C.: USGPO, December 1, 1989), p.113.

3. *Department of Defense Dictionary of Military and Associated Terms,* Joint Pub 1-02 (Washington, D.C.: USGPO, December 1, 1989), p.113.

4. In 1965 Secretary of Defense McNamara stated that, "the destruction of, say, one-quarter to one-third of its population and about two-thirds of its industrial capacity would mean the elimination of the aggressor as a major power for many years. Such a level of destruction would certainly represent intolerable punishment to any industrialized nation and thus should serve as an effective deterrent." With this statement, Secretary McNamara identified his interpretation of the type of deterrent threat that should be effective against "any industrialized nation." Quoted from, U.S. Senate, Committee on Armed Services and the Subcommittee on Department of Defense of the Committee on Appropriations, *Statement of Secretary Robert S. McNamara before the Committee on Armed Services and the Subcommittee on Department of Defense of the Committee on Appropriations, Hearings on Military Authorization and Defense Appropriations for Fiscal Year 1966,* 89th Congress, 1st Session, February 24, 1965, see pp. 42-46.

5. There is some indication that Russian analysts recognize the need to review past concepts of deterrence given some of the prominent features of the post-Cold War era. Retired Russian General Mikhail Vingradov recently observed that, "The events in the Persian Gulf have shown that the presence of totalitarian regimes in certain countries, and ethnic and religious strife between peoples of several states as well as in inside them, can lead and have already led to armed conflict and even war. Wars of such a nature belong to the category of unpreventable because in these cases the system of global nuclear deterrence does not work." Quoted from, *Report by the Coordinator of the 1st Section at the Plenary Session of the Conference on the Problems of the Global System of Protection,* Moscow, November 22, 1993, p.3 (mimeograph).

6. This brief discussion of psychological defense mechanisms is drawn from, Keith B. Payne and Lawrence Fink, "Deterrence Without Defense: Gambling on Perfection," *Strategic Review* (Winter 1989), p. 26.

7. For a basic discussion of psychological defense mechanisms such as repression and denial, William N. Dember and James J. Jenkins, *General Psychology: Modeling Behavior and Experience* (Englewood Cliffs, NJ: Prentice-Hall, 1970), pp. 659-678; and Lee Roy Beach, *Psychology: Core Concepts and Special Topics* (New York: Holt, Rinehart and Winston, 1973), pp. 187-198.

8. See, Group for the Advancement of Psychiatry, Committee on Social Issues, *Psychiatric Aspects of the Prevention of Nuclear War,* Report No. 57 (September, 1964), p. 241.

9. Peter Karsten, Peter D. Howell, and Artis Frances Allen, *Military Threats: A Systematic Historical Analysis of the Determinants of Success* (Westport, Conn., Greenwood Press, 1984), p. 21; Richard Lebow, "Miscalculation in the South Atlantic: The origins of the Falklands War," in Robert Jervis, Richard Ned Lebow, Janice Stein, *Psychology and Deterrence* (Baltimore: Johns Hopkins University Press, 1985), pp. 103, 119; and, in the same text, Lebow, "The Deterrence Deadlock: Is there a Way Out." pp. 182-183.

10. It is, for example, not clear if or how the apparent perpetrators of the March 19th sarin CW attacks in Tokyo subway trains could have been deterred. The motives and goals of Shoko Asahars and the "Aum Supreme Truth" Buddhist sect seem so obscure at this point that identifying an effective deterrent to these attacks may essentially have been impossible.

11. Quoted in, Peter Karsten, Peter Howell, and Artis Frances Allen, op. cit., p. 97.

12. See Don Oberdorfer, "Missed Signals In the Middle East," *The Washington Post Magazine,* March 17, 1991, p. 39.

13. Misinterpretation of an opponent's intentions occurs frequently in both military and economic relations, and in both cases typically leads to unanticipated actions on the part of the opponent. Such misjudgments can occur even following years of close interaction between the opponents. For example, Oleg Gordievski, a former senior Soviet intelligence officer has reported that in 1983 Soviet intelligence misinterpreted U.S. actions and intentions, and concluded that NATO was actively preparing to launch a massive sur[prise attack, including the use of nuclear weapons. See Grodon Brook-Shepard, *The Storm birds* (New York: Wiedenfeld and Nicolson, 1989), pp. 329-335. For an example of how misinterpretation of intentions has affected recent U.S.-Japanese trade discussions, see David E. Sanger,

"Missed Signals in Car War: U.S. and Japan Admit Misjudgments," *International Herald Tribune*, June 8, 1885, pp. 1, 6.

14. Stanford University Professor Alexander George is a prominent authority concerning deterrence and history. Quoted in , "Speaking with Alexander George about Coercive Diplomacy," *United States Institute of Peace Journal*, October 1991, p. 2. For a useful summary of Professor George's work, see, Alexander George, *Forceful Persuasion* (Washington, D.C.: U.S. Institute of Peace, 1991).

15. A critical problem with this strategy {deterrence} is that it rests on the assumption of pure rationality on the part of the opponent, and on his ability to recognize and act upon his self-interest. Of course, this assumption is inadequate—you must know the other side well enough to understand, in the particular case, the political, psychological, and cultural aspects of rationality." quoted in, "Speaking with Alexander George about 'Coercive Diplomacy,'" *op. cit.*, p.2.

16. Peter Karsten, Peter Howell, and Artis Frances Allen, op.cit., p. xii. Another prominent analyst of deterrence threats arrives at a similar conclusion: "Research to date indicates that the utility of deterrence is limited to a narrow range of conflicts: those in which adversarial leaders are motivated largely by the prospect of gain rather than by the fear of loss, have the freedom to exercise restraint, are not misled by grossly distorted assessments of the political-military situation, and are vulnerable to the kinds of threats that a would-be-deterrer is capable of credibly making. Deterrence must be practiced early on, before an adversary commits itself to a challenge and becomes correspondingly insensitive to warnings that such a course of action is likely to result in disaster. Unless these conditions are met, deterrence will be ineffective or counterproductive." From, Ned Lebow, "Deterrence Failure Revisited," *International Security* (Summer 1987), pp. 212-213.

17. See for example, Peter Karsten, Peter D. Howell and Artis Frances Allen, op cit; Robert Jervis, Richard Ned Lebow, Janice Stein, *Psychology and Deterrence* (Baltimore, MD; Johns Hopkins University Press, 1985; and Richard Ned Lebow, *Between Peace and War* (Baltimore, MD; Johns Hopkins University Press, 1981),p. 110; Raoul Naroll, Vern L. Bullogh, Frada Naroll, *Military Deterrence In History: A Pilot Cross-Historical Survey* (Albany, N.Y.: State University of New York Press, 1974), pp. 342-343.

18. Akiva Eldar, "Saddam would have Reason to Worry Says Arens When Asked about Unconventional Weapons," *Ha 'aretz,* February 4, 1991.

19. As discussed by Shai Feldman of Tel Aviv University's Jaffee Center for Strategic Studies and Amatzia Baram of Haifa University in their respective papers presented at a conference by the United States Institute of Peace, *Regional Stability in the Middle East: Arab and Israeli Concepts of Deterrence and Defense,* June 17-19, 1991, Washington, D.C.

20. *Baghdad INA,,* January 9, 1991, translated and presented in "INA reports Minutes of 'Aziz-Baker Meeting," FBIS-NES-92-009, January 14, 1992, p.27.

21. Reprinted in, *U.S. Department of State Dispatch, Persian Gulf,* January 14, 1991.

22. *Public Statement of Richard B. Cheney Secretary of Defense, Volume IV, Historical Office,* Office of the Secretary of Defense, 1990.p. 2547.

23. See for example the discussion in, U.S. Army Concepts Analysis Agency, Strategy and Plans Directorate, *Chemical Deterrence (CHEMDET), Phase I—Historical Background,* June 1992.

✦Deterring the Acquisition, Exploitation, and Use of Weapons of Mass Destruction

LEON SLOSS

I was asked to examine the problem of deterring the use of chemical and biological weapons in the current strategic environment where the emphasis is on the threat from small states with limited nuclear, chemical, or biological weapons capabilities.[1]

Reasons for the current interest in deterrence of chemical and biological weapons are clear. The Cold War is over and the Soviet threat has receded. Meanwhile, other states have acquired or seek to acquire weapons of mass destruction (WMD). Many turned first to chemical and/or biological weapons because the investment and

Leon Sloss is President of Leon Sloss and Associates, Chevy Chase, Maryland.

technological hurdles involved were far less than for nuclear weaponry. Compared to the massive intellectual and military effort expended on deterring the Soviet Union, relatively little thought has been given to how to deter these states from using their new capabilities. Furthermore, deterrence of chemical, and particularly, biological weapons, has received less attention than did nuclear weapons in the past. While it seems clear that deterring Iraq or Iran or North Korea will be different from deterring the Soviet Union, I argue here that the problems are by no means intractable. Nonetheless, there is a critical need to re-think the objectives of deterrence and the means by which they can be applied against these new threats.

Expanded Scope

While this paper focuses on deterring the use of chemical and biological weapons I have found it useful, and indeed necessary, to expand the inquiry in at least three dimensions:

First, the weapons to be deterred. In designing a deterrence strategy, the differences among countries are far more significant than the differences among weapons. Deterrence is directed at the actions of people and groups of people (i.e., governments), not at weapons themselves. Thus, while differences among chemical, biological, and nuclear weapons are pronounced, and will have a profound impact on military planning, the focus here is on deterrence, not fighting. The broad approaches to deterring a given country or leader from using such weapons are likely to be similar, if not identical, regardless of the weapon.

Second, the activities to be deterred. The interest of the U.S. Department of Defense in deterring *use* of chemical, biological, and nuclear weapons is understandable; it is a primary Pentagon mission. However, I contend that deterring their use is closely linked first, to deterring acquisition, and also relates to deterring exploitation of a nuclear, chemical or biological capability for purposes of influence, coercion, blackmail or—most importantly—to deter the United States. I will explore these linkages later.

Third, the countries to be deterred. Current U.S. Government attention focuses on proliferators—states that have recently acquired or are now seeking chemical, biological or nuclear weapons. We have already devoted substantial study to deterring Russia's use of WMD, but that cause is less urgent today than in the past. China, on the other hand, may have growing salience as its military power grows. Further, the problem of dealing with threshold WMD capabilities, such as Japan's, will require increasing attention.

In any case, what we learn about deterring proliferators may help us understand better how to deter other states, including the Russia of the future. And it is Russia that still poses the single most potent military threat to the United States. Russia today possesses by far the largest arsenal of nuclear weapons and long range missiles as well as substantial stocks of chemical and biological weapons.

Overview

The next section of the paper concerns principles of deterrence and expands upon the three categories just mentioned. I attempt to demonstrate what has changed and what has not changed in these principles of deterrence since the end of the Cold War.

I then develop these general principles for application to the central problem of the paper—what is required to deter the use of chemical and biological weapons by proliferators; i.e., countries other than former Soviet states and China. I discuss the four essential requirements for effective deterrence: a) a clear definition of U.S. security interests; b) detailed political, cultural, economic and military information about prospective adversaries; c) credible military capabilities and d) a demonstrated will to use available military capabilities.

The paper closes with a suggestion for organizing the U.S. Government to cope with proliferation and a comment on *no first use* in the new strategic setting.

About Deterrence

Who, What and How?

Whom are we deterring? When one reflects on deterrence, it soon becomes obvious that its target is not weapons, but *people*. More specifically, groups of people such as governments or regimes. The goal of deterrence is to discourage a group from using or threatening military force either by denying the user the results he seeks or by punishing him for his actions.

Different governments have different motives for wanting to acquire WMD, and may plan to use them in different ways. They will, therefore, respond in different ways to differing threats or to inducements employed to deter them. Deterrence is therefore a complex process that can require disparate approaches depending on the entity to be deterred. Generalizations do not suffice.

On the other hand, deterrent strategies designed to prevent acquisition, exploitation, and use of nuclear weapons in a given country are likely to apply to chemical and biological weapons as well, since we will presumably be dealing with the same leadership group that controls *all* WMD. Their motivations for threatening use of or using a weapon of mass destruction are likely to be similar be the weapon chemical, biological, or nuclear. It will be important to understand the goals of the potential aggressor if we are to effectively deny him those goals. It will also be important to understand the country's value system if we are to threaten punishment that really counts in its terms.

What do we seek to deter? Given the charter of the DOD in what has come to be known as "counterproliferation," there is understandable interest among those in the defense establishment in deterring *use* of WMD in war. Given the consequences of using WMD against U.S. forces, allies or the U.S. homeland, this represents the most dangerous threat.

But, deterring use is intimately linked with deterring acquisition, since, if it appears that it may be useful for a state to use or threaten to use a weapon, it will be motivated to acquire it. If use of a weapon is made to appear dangerous or counter-productive, the state or entity will be less likely to want to acquire it. We also have an interest in deterring use of mass destruction weapons of any kind, *short of war*, thus a broad deterrence strategy should be no less concerned with this type of "use."

Deterring exploitation of WMD. States may acquire nuclear, chemical or biological weapons without an intent to use them, or may find, once they have a nuclear, chemical or biological capability, that it would be very dangerous to use it in war, but that other, seemingly "attractive," uses, short of war, may exist. For example, states have acquired or sought to acquire nuclear and chemical weapons because their neighbors have them and they want to deter their neighbors' use.[2] Some states believe that having weapons confers prestige and influence, while others seek WMD as a deterrent to intervention by the United States or other powers from outside their region.[3] In this respect, some difference may exist between nuclear weapons when compared with chemical and biological weapons. States seem more inclined to brandish nuclear capabilities and to conceal chemical and biological weapons programs. This may be, in part, because the latter weapons can be more readily maintained in a latent state in peacetime and more rapidly mobilized in time of war.

These "uses" of a WMD capability short of war have received less attention than have either their acquisition or use. I believe they deserve more attention for several reasons: First, political uses are far more probable than military use. Second, it would hardly be conducive to stability if political purposes were to become an attractive or legitimate rationale for acquiring WMD, since once they are acquired the risk of use becomes far higher. Third, in many cases acquisition of WMD is directed against U.S. interests and will create new risks for the United States regardless of the intended or proclaimed purpose of the weapons. It should be a major goal of U.S. policy in this era of proliferation to prevent any state from using WMD to thwart the United States in pursuit of its security interests, including extension of deterrence to allies when we choose to do so.

Deterring Expansion of WMD Stockpiles. There is yet another reason for focusing on how a regime may "use" weapons of mass destruction short of militarily. Initial acquisition of a nuclear, chemical, or biological capability by a country is bad news, indeed. But expansion of that initial capability is much worse news.

Here, differences among the various forms of WMD become significant. More frequently cited differences include lethality, cost of development, ease of use on the battlefield, logistic support, and verification of the existence of stockpiles. There are also significant differences in past U.S. approaches to deterrence of nuclear, chemical, and biological use. Nuclear threats have always called for deterrence in kind. Chemical threats were treated in much the same way until very recently when the United States decided to eliminate an active retaliatory capability in order to encourage others to do the same. The United States never really developed BW as a deterrent and dropped all offensive programs after adhering to the 1969 BW Convention.

Differences in *military* utility not often discussed include the reality that a relatively modest and easily acquired stockpile of chemical weapons can have utility on the battlefield in a number of ways: it can deny certain areas to enemy forces for a period of time and it can slow the pace of operations by forcing an enemy to take protective measures. A small stockpile of nuclear weapons can be a powerful deterrent, but would be difficult to use to tactical advantage, particularly against a superior force. A nation with a small nuclear stockpile will always be faced with a dilemma. Use of a few weapons will have but modest military effect, particularly against a superior adversary. And, if a nation uses its weapons, it loses its deterrent. In this circumstance, the leadership is likely to find use of weapons for military effect a poor choice. As the weapons stockpile expands, strategic choices expand. Thus, the United States has a strong interest in deterring the expansion of stocks of WMD, particularly nuclear weapons.

Defining Deterrence

This chapter is about deterrence. Consequently, it is important to define what deterrence is. The concept of deterrence has been around a long time, and thus it is surprising that so much confusion remains in current literature about the relationship between deterrence and war fighting. *There is a strong link between deterrence and war fighting capabilities, but they are not identical.*

Discussions of deterrence frequently focus on what targets you must destroy and what weapons you must use in order to deter. These considerations are not irrelevant, but too little attention is paid in deterrence analyses to questions of whom you need to influence, and how. I have already noted that deterrence seeks to influence peoples' actions by threats of future action.

Thus, *the best deterrent is an unused deterrent.* Once a deterrent force is used, you are no longer in the business of initial deterrence, although you may be trying to restore it. More likely, you want to punish an adversary for having caused deterrence to fail.

An effective deterrent must be seen by an adversary as a force capable of doing what you have said it will do to deter him. Critically important to deterrence is an adversary's *perception* of your capabilities, not your actual capabilities. While it is impossible to deter with non-existent capabilities, deterrence frequently does involve bluffs or deception. Furthermore, military officials tend to be conservative, which leads to a tendency to view one's own capabilities skeptically and to exaggerate the other fellow's capabilities.

Writing in 1962, Tom Schelling said,

> Deterrence involves decisions that are based on beliefs and expectations. . . . Many national leaders . . . react to a mixture of impressions in which present and future capablities are confused, conflicting allegations are intuitively resolved and emphasis is determined by jounralism and political debate as much as by competent military evaluation.[4]

There are differences in how one measures a deterrent capability and a war fighting capability. The military are inclined to measure their own fighting capability in very conservative terms, and rightly so. If a leader is going to commit soldiers to battle he wants all the fighting power he can muster, and he wants to measure his capabilities by conservative criteria.

Measuring a deterrent capability is different. A deterrent is designed to influence an adversary's *perceptions* of your capabilities. Thus, you should measure your own deterrence capability in terms of how you believe the other side perceives it, not how you assess it. If the other side is also composed of conservative military folks, they will also tend to be conservative in their assessments, and thus will be likely to exaggerate your capability. This does not argue that deterrence can be achieved "on the cheap," but rather is a reminder of how one ought to measure a deterrent compared with measuring a war fighting capability.

Will and credibility are equally important to deterrence. By now it has become a truism that military capabilities alone are not sufficient. There also must be the *will* to use your capabilities. Again, what counts in deterrence is the other side's perception of your will to act, and this stems from actions you have taken or not taken over a long period of time. Referring again to Schelling, he says, commitments that matter are not simply those that are legally assumed, as in a treaty. Our commitment to react to a Soviet invasion of Germany does not mainly lie in a treaty obligation; it mainly lies in what we would lead the Soviets to believe, and what we would lead other countries to believe, if we did not react."[5] These perceptions or beliefs result from a pattern of actions by the deterrer over a period of months and years that build a reputation with respect to the use of force.

Deterrence Yesterday and Today

We have used several mechanisms for deterrence in the past when our principal adversary was the Soviet Union, the principal threat was nuclear, and the core of our deterrent was nuclear. Today's threats are more diverse and our deterrence policy must of necessity differ from that of the 1970s and 1980s. Nevertheless, it may be instructive to examine the deterrence mechanisms of the past to assess what may be applicable today and what may not be.

Retaliation in Kind: You attack me and I'll destroy you.

This was the earliest and the simplest form of deterrence in the nuclear era. When the U.S had superiority it made sense to threaten massive retaliation, and that was indeed the foundation of U.S. deterrent policy in the 1950s. Declaratory policy was never very specific concerning targets, but the assumption was that retaliation would be visited on cities. In fact, as the U.S. nuclear stockpile grew during the 1950s the targets became more diverse. But as we neared the end of that decade, it also became clear that superiority would be a fleeting asset. The Kennedy administration concluded that when the Soviet Union could essentially do to us what we could do to them, other options were needed—particularly more non-nuclear options.[6]

Today, one might think that the threat of massive retaliation would again be a logical and credible deterrent because the United States enjoys substantial nuclear superiority *vis-a-vis* small states with limited WMD stockpiles. However, a number of problems would pertain if massive retaliation were employed as a deterrent today.

First, the United States does not have a military stockpile of BW agents nor a weaponized CW stockpile. If we are to threaten retaliation against CW or BW use with existing capabilities, it must be either with nuclear or conventional weapons. In most circumstances, a nuclear response would appear excessive and might not be credible, while threat of a conventional weapon response might not be enough to deter. Neither threat might appear plausible to an adversary.

Second, and compounding the problem of plausibility, we have adopted a declaratory policy that appears to rule out the use of nuclear weapons against non-nuclear states even though they may possess, and even use, other weapons of mass destruction.[7] It may be argued, and some do, that an aggressor cannot be sure of our response despite declaratory policy. But it hardly seems a robust basis for deterrence to rely on an adversary not believing what you say.

Third, others contend that it is immoral for the United States to use nuclear weapons against a small state even if that state possesses or uses WMD.

Fourth, yet others assert that for the United States to retaliate with WMD against a very limited use of WMD by another state would constitute a further breach of a non-use taboo and thereby exacerbate the violation. The totality of this actual and declaratory posture has undermined the threat of retaliation by the United States as a deterrent against the use of chemical and biological weapons.

Counterforce Deterrence: If you attack, you will disarm yourself. In the early 1960s, when the United States perceived that the Soviets might achieve parity and be able to do unto us what we had heretofore only been able to do unto them, the appeal of massive retaliation waned. It was replaced by a counterforce doctrine, although countervalue still remained an "ace in the hole."

While counterforce was designed, in the first instance, to limit damage, it also had a deterrent role, particularly when combined with increasingly invulnerable forces. The deterrent threat of counterforce went something like this: *If you attack us you can do great damage, but in the end you will use up more weapons than you can destroy and then we, with your cooperation, will disarm you.* The threat was made more credible by the improved accuracy of weapons, by MIRVs, and by the hardening and deceptive basing of missiles.

The problem was that to prove the point required heroic assumptions and massive calculations. Sometimes the calculations proved the point and sometimes they didn't; it depended on the assumptions. In the end, deterrence was maintained primarily by the great uncertainties and the massive risks involved in being wrong.

Today, counterforce as a deterrent doctrine is limited by the fact that weapons of mass destruction are relatively easy to hide and difficult to find. The Chinese learned early on how to protect a small nuclear force through mobility and deceptive basing. Many of the new nuclear states seem to have learned the Chinese lesson, and in fact, many now have Chinese missiles accompanied by advisors.

Biological and chemical weapons are even easier to hide than nuclear weapons because the production facilities can dissolve into the civilian economy and delivery systems can be scattered among general purpose forces. Thus, a proliferator can undertake relatively inexpensive measures that can complicate counterforce targeting and may serve to convince him that counterforce threats are not credible.

Defense Emphasis: Our defenses can greatly complicate your attack and it may fail.. For a brief period in the 1980s, the United States seemed to be turning to a doctrine of defense emphasis. President Reagan had a vision of increasingly competent defenses supplanting deterrence. However, the best that most experts can promise for defenses is that they can complicate the calculations of a potential attacker and thereby contribute to deterrence by enlarging the uncertainty.

Improving forces' ability to operate effectively in a CBW environment can also contribute to deterrence. Adopting defenses such as improved battlefield detection measures, protective gear and rapid medical treatment that minimize the impact of CW and BW attacks on forces, and training forces in their use can convey much the same deterrent effect as active defenses. If the attacker believes you are prepared and are able to overcome or neutralize his use of WMD, he is less likely to use it. Training in proper doctrine and tactics also can contribute to deterrence. Like defenses, doctrine, and tactics are unlikely to be effective as stand-alone deterrents, but they can usefully supplement other means of deterrence.

International Opprobrium: If you use WMD—or acquire WMD contrary to international treaty—you will become a pariah. The United States and other states have made extensive efforts to deter use of nuclear, biological, and chemical weapons by placing them in the special category of WMD and by creating international legal strictures on their possession and use. The Geneva Convention of 1925 was an early effort to outlaw the use of chemical weapons. The NPT, the CWC and the Biological Weapons Treaty represent more recent efforts to generate international pressures against WMD acquisition and use.

The United States has employed extensive diplomatic pressure to influence states not to develop such weapons and to persuade those that have begun NBC weapons programs to abandon them. Efforts have been successful on several occasions when the United States had substantial leverage and used it; e.g., in South Korea and Taiwan. Other times the United States had less leverage or chose not to use it; e.g., Israel, Pakistan. In several cases it appears likely that the prospect of international opprobrium was a factor, although not the primary one, that led states to abandon nuclear programs on their own initiative; e.g., Sweden, South Africa, and Argentina.

Given the international laws and practices that have accumulated around WMD, it is certain that any state using WMD in any form would face strong criticism from the international community and would be forced to contemplate the high probability of economic sanctions or even military responses to WMD use. Thus, international opprobrium should serve as a very important deterrent to both acquisition and use for most states in most circumstances. Unfortunately, the risk of WMD use arises from a few states and a few circumstances where the threat of international sanctions is less effective. It was not sufficient to prevent use of chemical weapons in the Iran-Iraq war nor use by Iraq against the Kurds. In sum, while the international legal and political regime represents an important deterrent to acquisition, exploitation, and use of chemical and biological weapons, history teaches that it is not sufficient.

Deterrence Today

I have already noted the broad changes that have occurred in the setting for deterrence since the days of the Cold War. Nonetheless, some of the principles of traditional or classic deterrence still apply. Deterrence still depends fundamentally on impressive military capabilities that can credibly deny an adversary his objectives or inflict severe punishment if that adversary uses his capabilities in ways that are adverse to U.S. interests. Deterrence also requires credible demonstration of the will to use those capabilities. I will comment on both of these "traditional" requirements. However, I also want to suggest two other elements that are important to deterrence today: a) the ability to project will depends on having clearly defined national objectives; and b) implementing a deterrent strategy requires that we have detailed information on the states we may wish to deter that extends well beyond traditional military intelligence.

a) The need to define national interests and objectives. It may sound trite, even banal, to say a nation needs to define its national interests and objectives, but it is an essential first step in establishing deterrence. During the Cold War it came to be accepted that the United States had a vital interest not only in preventing a nuclear attack on itself, but in defending allies from nuclear threat or attacks. The fact that these were widely perceived as vital U.S. interests, even by our adversaries, was an essential element in deterrence, for it was plausible that the United States would pay a high price, and even go to war, to defend those interests. The interests were underlined, not only by declaratory statements by high-level U.S. officials, but by deployment of U.S. forces and nuclear weapons to those areas (e.g., Western Europe, Japan, and South Korea) where the United States wanted to make clear the importance of its interests.

No such clarity about U.S. interests exists today, and it should not be expected that it will exist soon, for the challenges of today and the past are not comparable. In our far more complex world, challenges to U.S. interests vary widely in intensity. It is as damaging to the credibility of deterrence to overstate national interests as to understate them or to fail to state them clearly. If exaggerated statements of national interest are made, but are not supported, the credibility of all statements of national interest is called into question.

Today, the American public seems averse to undertaking foreign commitments, particularly where U.S. lives might be at stake. However, definition of national interests is a responsibility of the nation's leadership. A sharper, more consistent definition of U.S. interests will be essential if deterrence is to maintain any credibility. For example, preventing the proliferation of weapons of mass destruction has been described as among the highest priority national security objectives by the administration.[8] Yet when it became apparent that the cost of preventing proliferation in North Korea could become excessive and that little support was forthcoming for a robust stance from U.S. allies in the region, the U.S. Government sought a compromise solution.

Given the serious risks of pursuing a confrontation with North Korea and the lack of allied (notably South Korean) support, the diplomatic track adopted by the U.S. Government may have been the only prudent course, but not without costs.

The seriousness of U.S. non-proliferation policy had now been called into question. The message conveyed to the North Koreans and others was that preventing proliferation may be an important interest, but not one that the United States is necessarily going to war for. Such perceptions inevitably affect the U.S. Government's ability to deter WMD acquisition.

There is even considerable uncertainty at policy-making levels whether the United States would or should become engaged if weapons of mass destruction were used and U.S. forces were *not* directly involved. The critical question is how seriously U.S. interests are affected by the act of a state using nuclear, chemical or biological weapons. The U.S. decried the use of chemical weapons by Iraq against the Kurds, but that was the extent of U.S. action.

South Asia is a region where use of a nuclear weapons in war is at least conceivable. It is not a region where vital U.S. interests exist, but any use of nuclear weapons in war would seriously affect global stability and would impact U.S. interests. Is the United States prepared to intervene with force to prevent nuclear weapons (or chemical or biological weapons) from being used even if no direct interests are at stake? If so, what circumstances would lead the United States to intervene and what forms would that intervention take?

Even more pointedly, in a number of recent war games, questions have been raised as to whether the United States should retaliate with nuclear weapons if chemical or biological or even nuclear weapons themselves were used against U.S. forces.[9] Is the use of a nuclear, chemical or biological weapon against U.S. forces a cause for retaliation? Under what circumstances? Are there clear instances where the United States would retaliate and others where we would not? How might these instances be defined? Can the United States expect deterrence to work against a state with vital security interests in a particular region when U.S. interests there are less than vital? No one can expect precise formulation of U.S. interests and guidelines for U.S. intervention. Sometimes interests become clear only when they are directly challenged, as was the case when Iraq invaded Kuwait in 1990 or North Korea invaded South Korea in 1950. Still, greater clarity about U.S. interests and objectives is needed, or an essential basis for maintaining a credible deterrent will be lacking.

b) Creating credible will is a long-term proposition. It has long been accepted by strategists that demonstrated will to utilize force is an essential element of deterrence. While military capabilities required to establish deterrence have been analyzed at length over the decades, the "will" factor has received less attention.

It was understandable during the Cold War when U.S. will, if not taken for granted by all of our allies (e.g., De Gaulle), was at least manifest in many ways. There were a series of verbal commitments by U.S. leaders. President Kennedy's famous declaration at the Berlin Wall, "Ich bin ein Berliner," was one among many such declarations.

These statements of policy were underlined by treaty commitments such as the North Atlantic Treaty Organization and the Rio Treaty. Perhaps most importantly, they were further reinforced by deployment of hundreds of thousands of U.S. forces and thousands of nuclear weapons overseas. Today, many of these former symbols of U.S. will and commitment are lacking, and a set of different signals is being sent as forces and weapons are withdrawn from allied bases and alliances themselves are being attacked in the U.S. Congress.

The overall security posture and policies of a nation and its reputation, or track record, in the use of force to control aggression have an extremely important bearing on that nation's ability to deter another state. A nation can have overwhelming military power, but if an adversary perceives that this power is unlikely to be used, it will not deter.

That axiom has been dramatically illustrated in the current conflict in what was Yugoslavia. The will to deter is not a force that can be summoned on command like a squadron of attack aircraft. Political will and the reputation of a state are implanted in the mind of a future adversary by a series of actions taken over many years or decades. The actions may have little to do directly with weapons of mass destruction. For example, U.S. policies in the Balkans over the past three years have vacillated between tough threats and timid actions. Force has been applied before the next steps in the process have been thought out. There are a good many reasons for the twists and turns in U.S. policy in the region, however. Among the most realistically important is that the making of policy has not been entirely under U.S. control. Whatever the reasons, the recent Balkan experience has created an impression that the United States as a nation is confused about its goals and timid—in the extreme—in making a commitment of force.[10] These circumstances are bound to affect our credibility should we find it necessary to utilize force or threats of force to deter future WMD exploitation and use.

c) Capabilities still count, but perhaps not as much. Deterrence requires formidable military capabilities, but during a recent DOD effort to define a counterproliferation program, capabilities were overemphasized when compared with credible will. There is little doubt that the United States has formidable military capabilities and can retaliate against any nation that employs weapons of mass destruction. U.S. nuclear capability requires little elaboration; the question is to what extent that capability is relevant to deterring the use of chemical or biological weapons.

U.S. non-nuclear capabilities were demonstrated with awesome effect in the Persian Gulf War. Again, the question that affects deterrence is whether, and under what circumstances, the United

States would use these capabilities in the future. The absence of U.S. offensive capabilities in BW and CW, and the U.S. commitment not to produce them, makes their role in deterrence moot.

Requirements for military capabilities that are able to counter proliferation have been studied extensively by the Defense Department during the past three years, and there remains little I can add in a paper of this scope. However, I do want to comment briefly on defenses and on the role of nuclear weapons.

Defenses can deter. Most redent DOD studies have identified defenses as an important component of a counterproliferation capability. Among defensive capabilities that have high priority for development are theater missile defense (TMD), CW warning, BW warning, rapid inoculation and medical care, and improved protective gear.[11]

These emphases seems to me appropriate, not only as prudent measures to prepare for warfare, but also as ways to stiffen deterrence. Specifically, improved CW and BW defenses will contribute to deterrence in at least two ways. First, a serious program of CW and BW warning and defenses conveys the message that the United States takes seriously the need to be prepared to operate in a CW/BW environment. It also suggests to potential adversaries that the United States will not be readily deterred by CW or BW threats. Second, the stronger U.S. defensive capabilities are, the less certain an adversary can be that use of CW or BW use will be successful. As I noted earlier, the aggressor's uncertainty of success can be an element in deterrence. Improvements in BW and CW warning and in passive and active defenses will strengthen deterrence.

Nuclear weapons do have a role in deterrence of chemical and biological weapons threats. Some "authorities" argue that nuclear weapons can play no role in deterring chemical and biological use; that the only role of nuclear weapons is to deter other nuclear weapons.[12] At the other extreme are a few advocates of developing new nuclear weapons, such as earth penetrators, that perform such specific military missions as attacks on underground bunkers.[13]

Both views miss the point, it seems to me, when it comes to deterrence of BW/CW. Nuclear weapons will not have a central role to play in deterring CW or BW actions, since use of a nuclear weapon by the United States could only be justified if a critical threat to U.S. interests were posed. Thus, the credibility of a U.S. nuclear response to chemical or biological weapons use is destined to be somewhat suspect. Still, the use of nuclear weapons in retaliation should not be entirely ruled out. Today, it is possible to postulate a biological weapon threat of catastrophic proportions, either directed at deployed U.S. forces, civil populations, or both. No adversary can be allowed the impression that a major attack on U.S. forces or civilians would go unanswered or would receive a feeble response.

The *deterrence* role of nuclear weapons is not so exact that it can be tied to specific missions or targets. What we want to convey to any nation—and its leadership—that seeks to acquire, exploit, or use chemical or biological weapons is that consequences of its action would not only be incalculable, but potentially dangerously deleterious to its own objectives.

The sorts of vague threats of severe consequences that were employed by the United States Government to deter Saddam Hussein from using his chemical arsenal in 1990-91 serve as an example of how nuclear weapons may be used in deterrence. Many believe those subtle threats worked.

The fault with the argument by those who say nuclear weapons should never be used to deter a chemical or biological threat is that it removes a necessary element of uncertainty.

The problem with the argument that we need a particular new weapon to pose a credible threat is that it suggests that current U.S. military capabilities are not awesome enough to deter, a message neither accurate nor conducive to deterrence.

Theater nuclear weapons can play a role in deterring exploitation and use of chemical and biological weapons. If nuclear weapons are destined to have only a secondary or "back-up" role in deterrence, does it make much difference what kinds of weapons the United States retains for this role? I believe that it does. If we ever face an adversary that threatens the use of chemical or biological weapons against U.S. forces or allies, we must be able to demonstrate dramatically that the United States has the capability and the will to make consequences of such an action disastrous. We may want to "brandish" our nuclear capability in a very obvious fashion.

This is difficult to do with ICBMs because signs of increased readiness may not be obvious to an adversary that does not have sophisticated intelligence gathering systems. Submarines could be deployed near the threatened area, but again this would not be a visible demonstration of readiness. The most obvious signal could be delivered by forward deployment of strategic bombers. While these bombers do not actually require forward basing to operate at long distances, since they can be aerially refueled, their deployment to forward bases would send a stronger deterrence signal than would airborne patrols that come and go and remain invisible to all but sophisticated radar.

However, large, pre-stocked forward bases capable of handling strategic bombers may not always be available when and where needed. Thus, it would be useful for purposes of deterrence to retain the option to deploy nuclear-capable tactical air and ground forces to forward locations on short notice to demonstrate vividly that the United States intends to deter chemical, biological (or nuclear) threats.[14]

d) The need for detailed information on the goals and values, as well as the military assets, of target nations. Information has always been an essential element of deterrence. During the Cold War, a significant sector of the U.S. intelligence apparatus was directed at collecting information on the Soviet Union. Information sought included not only the data on order of battle required for targeting but also intelligence on doctrine, leadership, economics, and political structure. Similar knowledge is needed today on states that possess or seek to acquire weapons of mass destruction.

One frequently hears the comment that the new proliferators we deal with today may not be deterrable because their societies do not share our "Western" values. It is also claimed that their leaders are immune to threats of retaliation or their societies more readily accept risk than does our own. These arguments reflect the fact that we do not know *how* to deter those states, not necessarily that country X or leader Y cannot be deterred. While I do not minimize the problem of deterring new members of the nuclear, chemical, or biological weapons club, I would like to remind others that similar comments were made concerning the difficulty of understanding Soviet views of strategy in the 1950s. It was decades before we developed confidence in the proposition of mutual deterrence with the Soviet Union.

Deterring the use of chemical and biological weapons is difficult, but not impossible. To effectively deter proliferators we must study the society of a potential adversary intently to understand what motivates its leaders. Not only must we understand what motivates them to acquire WMD, what plans they have for weapons use, or how they will be deployed, but also how command and control of the weapons is organized and what assets or values are most critical to the society so we may evaluate a variety of deterrent threats. But that is a job for psychologists and sociologists, not for targeteers.

Each country we must deal with will require a tailored proliferation strategy; one suit will not fit all. It may sound like a formidable job, but we are talking about relatively few states that are both serious proliferation threats and that are in a position to seriously threaten important U.S. concerns. Efforts to develop such data are already underway in the intelligence community. They need continuing support, and results of intelligence gathering efforts must be fed continuously into military and diplomatic planning. In the final section of this paper I suggest an approach to accomplishing this goal.

A very different problem exists with respect to non-state actors that acquire WMD. Terrorists and other loosely organized groups may have no organized "core" or headquarters against which retaliation can be threatened. They may lack any coherent set of goals or beliefs which might provide a target for counteraction. Some groups may be quite immune to traditional deterrence concepts. In such cases denial or defenses may provide the only solution. Dealing with threats from such groups is likely to be the responsibility of police and paramilitary units rather than regular military formations.

Conclusions

Organizing to Deal with Proliferation

Too often counter-proliferation is discussed as an abstract, unitary problem. In the real world of government, where decisions must be made and actions taken, proliferation problems most frequently arise on a country-by-country or regional basis.

The suggestion here is that the U.S. Government develop a new series of counter-proliferation contingency plans for key countries or regimes where proliferation is a major issue. The plans would be the focal point for bringing to bear all of the government's resources, for developing specific non-proliferation policies and plans, for working out inter-agency differences and for identifying action responsibilities related to the differing phases of the plan. The proposal is based on the following assumptions:

- There are relatively few countries in which proliferation of weapons of mass destruction represents a major national security issue for the United States;

- U.S. policies and programs should focus heavily, not exclusively, on these countries;

- Each country will present a different problem and require different solutions (in some area, for example South Asia, the Middle East—the problem may be best addressed regionally);
- Interagency coordination will be essential, since no single agency has responsibility for the multiple facets of non/counter-proliferation policy;
- For interagency coordination to be effective, some organization is required. A plan can provide a focal point for coordination, and brings people from different agencies to work together;
- Developing contingency plans will assure more effective action if and when contingencies arise, since the people who will be working together in crises will have the opportunity to plan together beforehand.

It must be recognized, however, that the most careful advanced planning cannot anticipate all situations. Therefore, when a proliferation event occurs, plans must be adapted to the particular situation.

Plan Content

The plan for each country will differ, but all should include the following elements:

A *threat assessment* that summarizes the country's present and prospective capabilities related to weapons of mass destruction and delivery systems. As suggested above, equally important in a threat assessment is analysis of the country's values, goals, leadership, command organization, societal strengths and vulnerabilities, and so forth.

A *contingency assessment* that summarizes political and military contingencies that might arise within this country and the nature of possible U.S. involvement.

Deterrent actions that the United States might take to deter acquisition of weapons of mass destruction and related delivery systems.

Coping actions the United States might take if proliferation occurred, and a WMD was employed short of military action; e.g., to threaten or coerce a neighbor.

Military actions the U.S. might take to include requirements for developing and acquiring new capabilities in addition to those of military force.

An agenda for international cooperation that would spell out steps necessary for coordinating with other governments and international organizations.

How to Get Started

An effort of this sort should probably be initiated under National Security Council auspices, since it will require substantial coordination among several national security agencies. However, any among the national security agencies of State, Defense, or the CIA could initiate planning and call on others to join in. In the precedent that I will cite, the process was initiated by the State Department and ultimately brought under NSC auspices.

The first step in the process should be to identify countries that represent a sufficient threat, either political or military, to warrant an intensive interagency planning effort. It might be well to start with no more than a half-dozen countries. The second step would be to identify the kinds of situations or contingencies that might arise in each country that would be likely to require major U.S. policy decisions or actions. An inventory of existing intelligence estimates and contingency plans for these countries should be made. Interagency working groups should then fill in the gaps in planning.

Once initial plans have been developed an important role should be played by gaming to test and refine the plans. Path gaming, which looks at an issue over a protracted period of time, could be particularly useful.

A Precedent

There is a precedent for such a program. In the 1960s a series of interagency political-military contingency plans were developed under the leadership of the Department of State. Initially, there was strong bureaucratic resistance to the idea. Military planners did not want other agencies "reviewing" their contingency plans. Many State Department officers at desk level did not believe that operational planning was part of their portfolio. Intelligence officers resisted sharing sensitive intelligence. In time, these objections were overcome and some very good plans emerged. Several were put to use, for example, during the Soviet invasion of Czechoslovakia in 1968. Eventually this planning process was assumed by the Washington Special Action Group, an interagency committee set up by Henry Kissinger when he was national security advisor.

Non-proliferation presents a different set of issues, but the technique would seem to be adaptable to present day problems.

Reconsideration of No First Use

This paper has argued that nuclear weapons have a role to play in deterring acquisition, exploitation, and use of chemical and biological weapons, albeit a secondary or "back-up" role. Some strategists have suggested that amendment of U.S. declaratory policy with respect to so-called negative security assurances (NSA) would help to strengthen deterrence of chemical and biological threats.[15] They have proposed a policy of no first use against all weapons of mass destruction, leaving open the option for the United States to retaliate against chemical or biological use. This could help to strengthen CBW deterrence, but such a change in declaratory policy also presents some very serious pitfalls. Current policy preserves an option for first-use of nuclear weapons against a conventional attack supported by a nuclear power, but it strongly implies that a nuclear or chemical attack against the United States or a U.S. ally would not generate a nuclear response, provided the attacker was not a nuclear state and was a signatory to the NPT. According to critics, this policy is an outmoded legacy of the Cold War. It preserves a first-use option that was designed to deter a Soviet attack by superior conventional forces in Central Europe—a threat that no longer exists. On the other hand, it unduly constrains U.S. options to deter a real and growing threat from chemical and biological weapons.

Changing policy is always a tricky business and when the policy concerns nuclear weapons, it can be particularly sensitive. While the threat to Europe is greatly diminished, the United States must guard against the impression that it is altering its nuclear guarantee to its allies in Europe. This is particularly true now that the United States has withdrawn substantial forces from Europe, thereby creating uncertainty about U.S. intentions; when there have been frictions with allies over Bosnia; and as NATO is considering the delicate issue of expansion.

Changes in policy must also steer clear of sending the wrong signals to Russia when there is considerable political upheaval and uncertainty about the future course of Russian security policy. Futhermore, the non-nuclear parties to the NPT will be very sensitive to any changes in U.S. policy, particularly if they can be portrayed as challenging delicate bargains that paved the way for NPT renewal. Any change in U.S. nuclear policy could also be challenged by a Congress that is highly critical of the conduct of foreign policy by the Clinton administration.

Given these potential pitfalls, the time does not seem ripe for a formal change in U.S. declaratory policy. Recent public speculation about the role that U.S. nuclear weapons played in deterring Iraqi use of chemical and biological weapons in the 1991 Gulf War has created, what seems to this writer, a useful degree of ambiguity that enhances deterrence. It does not seem necessary to make any specific changes in declaratory policy to clarify this ambiguity at the present time. Trying to do so could be counterproductive.

The proposal by the RAND experts appeals to a typically American sense of clarity and order. For this reason it appealed to me on first reading. However, on reflection I prefer the more nuanced approach of a wise British expert, Sir Michael Quinlan who said:

> No one for decades past has seriously thought of using nuclear weapons save in defense of deeply vital interests where no other course would serve. It may, especially since 1991, be hard for the nuclear powers to see how their deeply vital interests are at all likely to be threatened by non-nuclear means that could not be countered in non-nuclear ways. But if in the end that expectation were confounded, and vital interests were indeed about to be overborne by non-nuclear means—chemical or biological attack, let us say, or trade strangulation—the idea that a nuclear power would let itself be overwhelmed simply because of a no first use declaration is plainly absurd. . . . To the extent that such a [no first use] declaration merely indicates preference and probability, it is unnecessary; to the extent that it purports to promise something more, it cannot be dependable. [16]

This may be seen by some as an argument for a declaratory policy of "no first use." However, it really is an argument for creative ambiguity, for in the very next sentence Quinlan goes on to say that *"It is ... doubtfully beneficial to weaken general deterrence of major war by purporting to remove entirely the helpful shadow of nuclear weapons."* [Emphasis added.] This seems to me to be just the right point at which to leave the matter of declaratory policy for now.

Notes

1.   This paper focuses on how to deter small and fractious states such as Iran, Iraq and North Korea. However, there are other states that present deterrence challenges for U.S. policy. Both Russia and China have nuclear, chemical and biological programs and face important decisions about whether to modify, expand or dismantle them. Other significant powers with WMD potential are Japan and Germany. The larger states cannot be ignored as the U.S. seeks to devise a new deterrent posture for the post-Cold War world.

2.   For example, the principal rationale for the Pakistani nuclear program has been the threat posed by India. Both Iran and Iraq acquired chemical weapons primarily to offset the other party's chemical weapons. Those states in the Middle East that have sought a nuclear capability (i.e., Iraq) or are now seeking such a capability (i.e., Iran) cite Israel's program as a rationale for their own programs.

3.   Following the Persian Gulf War in 1991, the Indian Defense Minister was widely quoted as saying that if any country wanted to prevent the U.S. from intervening in their region in the future they would need to have a nuclear capability.

4.   "Strategic Developments Over the Next Decade," a draft report prepared by a study group under Prof. Thomas Schelling for an Interagency Panel, October 1962.

5.   Ibid.

6.   See William W. Kaufman, *The McNamara Strategy*, Chapter 2, "The Search for Options."

7.   U.S. policy on negative security assurances was announced in the United Nations on June 12, 1978 and has never been formally renounced. The key passage of that statement says, "The United States will not use nuclear weapons against any non-nuclear weapons state party to the NPT . . . except in the case of an attack on the United States, its territories or armed forces, or its allies, by such a state allied to a nuclear weapons state . . . in carrying out or sustaining the attack."

8.   *"One of our most urgent priorities must be attacking the proliferation of weapons of mass destruction whether they are nuclear, chemical or biological, and the ballistic missiles that can rain them down on populations hundreds of miles away. ...If we do not stem the proliferation of*

the world's deadliest weapons, no democracy can feel secure." President Bill Clinton in a speech to the United Nations General Assembly, September 1993.

9. See "The Day After ... Study - Nuclear Proliferation in the Post-Cold War World;" Marc Dean Millot, Roger Molander, Peter A. Wilson; The RAND Corporation, 1993, p. 15.

10. In recent meetings in Europe the author was confronted with frequent questions about the "Powell doctrine," which was seen by Europeans as requiring overwhelming U.S. superiority before the U.S. would commit military force, thereby making such commitment much less likely.

11. See "Report on Nonproliferation and Counterproliferation Activities and Programs," Office of the Deputy Secretary of Defense, May 1994.

12. See, for example, Lewis Dunn, "Rethinking the Nuclear Equation: The United States and the New Nuclear Powers," *The Washington Quarterly*, Winter 1994.

13. See, for example, Thomas W. Dowler and Joseph S. Howard,"Stability in a Proliferated World," *Strategic Review*, Spring 1995.

14. For a further discussion of the role of TNF in counterproliferation, see "A World Without Theater Nuclear Weapons," by Leon Sloss for the Institute of National Strategic Studies, May 1995.

15. For a clearly articulated argument on no-first-use of WMD, See "U.S. Nuclear Declaratory Policy: The Question of Nuclear First Use," by David Gompert, Kenneth Watman and Dean Wilkening, The RAND Corporation, 1995.

16. *British Nuclear Weapons Policy: Past, Present and Future* by Sir Michael Quinlan in "Strategic Views from the Second Tier: The Nuclear Weapons Policies of France, Britain and China," edited by John C. Hopkins and Weixing Wu, University of California, institute on Global Conflict and Cooperation, 1993.

✦ ABOUT THE EDITOR

Dr. Stuart Johnson is currently the Chief Scientist, Naval War College. Previously he was the Director of Strategy and Policy Analysis, Institute for National Strategic Studies. In 1988, he was appointed Director of Regional Studies of the Institute. This group was established by the Secretary of Defense and the Chairman of the Joint Chiefs of Staff to do long-range studies of key national security issues. Dr. Johnson was also an Adjunct Professor of Defense Policy and Program Analysis at the George Washington University's School of International Affairs in Washington, DC.

Dr. Johnson graduated from Amherst College, where he was selected for Phi Beta Kappa. He received his Ph.D. from the Massachusetts Institute of Technology, after which he spent a year as a NATO Fellow at the University of Leiden in the Netherlands.

*U.S. G.P.O.:1996-405-201:40017